# Living
# JOURNALISM

## principles & practices
## for an essential profession

## Rich Martin

UNIVERSITY OF ILLINOIS AT URBANA–CHAMPAIGN

**Holcomb Hathaway, Publishers**
*Scottsdale, Arizona*

Library of Congress Cataloging-in-Publication Data

Martin, Rich.
  Living journalism : principles & practices for an essential profession /
Rich Martin.
     p. cm.
  Includes index.
  ISBN 978-1-934432-22-8
  1. Journalism—Handbooks, manuals, etc.   2. Journalism—Technique.
I. Title.
  PN4775.M382 2011
  808'.06607—dc23

                                                          2011020499

Holcomb Hathaway, Publishers, Inc.
8700 E. Via de Ventura Blvd., Suite 265
Scottsdale, Arizona 85258
480-991-7881
www.hh-pub.com

ISBN PRINT: 978-1-934432-22-8
ISBN EBOOK: 978-1-934432-21-1

Printed in the United States of America.

# contents

I had a master's degree in English but no job. Desperate, I thought that maybe I could be a reporter. But the big newspaper in Atlanta only wanted people with experience, and a suburban paper turned me down for the same reason. Then I saw an ad for a police and courts reporter at *The Gwinnett Daily News* in my hometown. I called and was invited in for an interview.

The editors asked me a lot of questions and then gave me some facts that I was to use to write a police brief. I made my deadline, but it was agonizing. My story looked like the kind you'd see in the paper, but I wasn't sure if I had missed a trap that had been laid for me. I must have done all right, though. I got the job. I was going to be a newspaper reporter.

I had no clue about how much I didn't know.

Billy Williams helped me learn. A cigar-smoking veteran reporter, he introduced me to police officers, detectives and, importantly, the clerks and assistants who knew what was really going on. Billy chatted with everyone, asking about them and their families and, of course, about anything interesting that might have happened overnight. He showed me where to look for police reports and court records, and he taught me how to conduct myself when I covered a trial: dress well, be on time, sit in the front row, take careful notes, ask questions afterward, get everything right.

Over the next months I went out with him on stories and watched him work. He asked hard questions, but he always treated people with respect. I marveled at the seeming ease with which he wrote his stories. They had punchy leads, while mine were long-winded. His stories said exactly what they needed to say, and nothing more. He wasn't Hemingway, but he had studied writing and knew that less is often more.

Billy Williams probably never thought of himself as a mentor. I certainly didn't think of him that way during my first year as a reporter. But as I got more experience—learning journalism by practicing it in the company of many other talented reporters and editors—I came to appreciate what Billy did for me. He gave advice when I asked for it—and sometimes when I didn't—and he offered constructive criticism when I needed it. He was generous with his time and his interest. He exemplified the essential standards that are key to journalism, and had confidence that I would pick up some of the things he wanted me to learn. I was lucky to work with him.

The best journalists care about the nurturing of new journalists. The veterans remember the people who trained them, and they want to give something back to a younger generation. Journalism is a fragile craft; practiced carelessly, it reflects poorly on both the individual practitioner and other journalists as well. The veterans recall the mistakes they made when they started out, and they want young journalists to avoid making the same mistakes or, at minimum, to learn from mistakes when they are made and not repeat them. They know that the best habits and values are instilled early in one's career.

Journalism has changed a lot since I first entered a newsroom, and even since I started teaching journalism to college students in 2005. News is faster, thanks to the Internet and the mobile devices and applications that keep us connected 24/7. Many people still rely on their daily printed newspaper, but they are likely to visit its website for the latest news. Others rely on the web exclusively.

Some things about journalism haven't changed, though, and shouldn't. Many fundamental standards have stood the test of time, and they still apply in today's fast, digital world. *Living Journalism* is about those core values and practices that beginning journalists must develop if they are to produce work that informs and enlightens citizens. Each of its sixteen chapters deals with key principles that journalists need to embrace, such as developing a curious and skeptical mind, asking good questions, paying attention to details and preparing for the unexpected. The book challenges journalists to provide a voice for people without influence and to act as a watchdog over those who do have power. It emphasizes the importance of developing a moral compass that will provide guidance for the ethical challenges that all journalists face in their careers.

Good journalistic mentors are as important now as they ever were, but it may be more difficult today to find a Billy Williams who will serve in that role. This book allows readers to learn from the experiences of reporters and editors at news organizations around the country. Based on research and dozens of interviews, it includes the advice and stories of professionals who can serve as mentors, even if they aren't able to physically sit beside readers and teach them first-hand. As readers learn the values and practices they need to know to perform their jobs responsibly and thoroughly, they will see examples of how the best journalists exemplify fundamental principles. They will also understand how those principles still apply today, no matter which platform is used to produce and present the news. Readers will discover how experienced journalists go about their jobs, how they learned to do their work accurately and honestly, and the lessons they have learned from the mistakes that all journalists inevitably make during their careers.

The best journalists know that solid reporting practices and values are developed only through experience, and *Living Journalism* is designed to encourage readers to act on what they've learned. Chapters include exercises that encourage readers to go beyond the book, sending them into their own communities to practice new skills and to develop expertise. Some of the exercises are challenging, but all are designed to foster learning and understanding of the fundamentals needed to excel as journalists in the twenty-first century.

The beginning journalists who follow the fundamental standards and examples of the people profiled in this book can eventually become mentors themselves for the next generation of journalists, passing along the values and practices that must survive. That may be their most important legacy.

# acknowledgments

Most journalists have the privilege of working with many talented and experienced people. I have been particularly blessed in this regard. Some of the people I learned from are mentioned in this book, but many are not. Bob Wynn, Gainer Bryan and Bob Fowler gave me my first job; instead of firing me after I made a mistake on my first published story they helped me learn from it. Forrest Landon, Ben Bowers and Barton Morris gave me early opportunities at *The Roanoke Times*. I am forever indebted to all the reporters, editors, photographers, artists and other news staffers I worked with at that paper. I can't name them all.

Thanks also to the people who talked to me about their work as young and experienced journalists. Their commitment to journalism and its values serves as a shining example for the young journalists who will use this book.

My colleagues in the Department of Journalism at the University of Illinois come from a variety of journalism backgrounds, but all of them hold dear the fundamental values that I write about in this book. Thanks to them for the example they set for our students and for their support of my work.

I extend my sincere thanks to the following individuals, who reviewed my text and offered invaluable suggestions for its improvement: Michael Bugeja, Iowa State University; Andrew R. Cline, Missouri State University; Meredith Cummings, University of Alabama; Brian Richardson, Washington and Lee University; Jocelyn Steinke, Western Michigan University; Carl Sessions Stepp, University of Maryland; and Wayne A. Worcester, University of Connecticut.

Lauren Salas, my editor at Holcomb Hathaway, Publishers, believed in this book from the beginning. Thanks for your support and your editing.

Margaret, my wife, kept me going when I couldn't even imagine the ending. Thanks for your love and confidence.

Finally, my great appreciation to Billy Williams. I left the *Gwinnett Daily News* after a year to travel in Europe. Billy and I shook hands and he wished me well. When I returned to the States, he was no longer at the paper. I never saw him or spoke to him again. I am filled with regret that I never gave him the thanks that he deserved. For now, this is the best I can do.

## CHAPTER 1

What can I say about journalism? It has the greatest virtue and the greatest evil. It is the first thing a dictator controls. It is the mother of literature and the perpetrator of crap. In many cases it is the only history we have and yet it is the tool of the worst men. But over a long period of time and because it is the product of so many men, it is perhaps the purest thing we have. Honesty has a way of creeping into it even when it was not intended.

JOHN STEINBECK,
IN A 1956 LETTER[1]

# you've got to be a little crazy

Photojournalist Igor Kostin and his pilot approached the Chernobyl nuclear power plant after a 45-minute helicopter flight from Kiev, Ukraine.[2] Military vehicles scurried around on the ground, and then suddenly everything seemed to stop. In front of him, Kostin saw a large hole "like an open grave." The roof of the plant's No. 4 reactor, a 3,000-ton slab of concrete, had been blown off by an explosion.

"I saw the colors and the unbelievable light," said Kostin, the first photojournalist on the scene. He had never seen anything like it before. No one else had, either.

His helicopter circled 150 feet above the glowing reactor, while Kostin shot pictures of what soon became the worst nuclear accident in history. His camera jammed after twenty or thirty shots. A second camera also malfunctioned, its motor destroyed by radiation. Back in Kiev, Kostin developed his film but only the first six or seven exposures survived; everything else was black. He sent the most acceptable photo to his news agency, but the Soviet government suppressed early reports of the accident and blocked the photo's publication.

The accident at Chernobyl on April 26, 1986, seems like a long time ago, but its effects are still felt today. The explosion spewed radiation over large portions of northern Europe and what was then the Soviet Union. At least 31 people were killed by radioactivity within two months, and hundreds of thousands of people were permanently displaced. The United Nations estimates that 10,000 people will ultimately die from cancers caused by radiation from the explosion, but groups such as Greenpeace insist the final toll could be ten times higher.

Kostin went back again and again to document what happened at Chernobyl. His news agency was willing to let him return, but it would not provide him a car. "You do not understand," his superiors told him. "A journalist is replaceable, but a car. . . ."

Kostin felt ill every time he returned to his home in Kiev. To counter the effects of the radiation on his thyroid, he was told to drink vodka—half a glass for every two hours spent at the disaster site. It made little sense, but he followed the prescribed regimen anyway. In early 1987 he went to a military hospital in Moscow and received blood transfusions that made him feel a little better. Photographs were not permitted, but Kostin smuggled a camera in and took pictures of other patients who had been contaminated by radiation from Chernobyl.

Chernobyl became Kostin's life work. "I felt that history was being played out, and that someone had to devote themselves to it seriously," he said in 2006. "My pictures are like an instruction manual for the next generation, so that something like it can never happen again."

Igor Kostin might strike you as crazy. He would probably agree. Journalism, he has said, is a profession "not for normal people." He doesn't mean that as an insult to journalists or to normal people. He means that journalists rush to the scene of the nuclear accident or the burning building to get the story. Normal people head the other way.

Some may find Kostin's notion peculiar, romantic or even arrogant. After all, while professional journalists have learned their craft and honed their skills over many years, many believe that anyone can be considered a journalist. In fact, that is what "citizen journalists" do today, using websites, blogs, YouTube videos and Twitter to independently report events in their neighborhood and around the world. For example, Janis Krums, a 24-year-old businessman from Sarasota, Florida, was on a New York ferry when US Airways Flight 1549 crash landed in the Hudson River in January 2009. Using his iPhone, Krums took a picture of the plane resting on the river's surface and posted it to Twitter. It was the first photo of the crash scene. "There's a plane in the Hudson," Krums Tweeted. "I'm on the ferry going to pick up the people. Crazy." Within a half hour of posting his photo, Krums was giving an eyewitness report of the crash to MSNBC.

Citizen accounts such as Krums's are not new. They were the life-blood of the early days of American journalism, albeit created with different tools. Today we use phones, laptop computers and other Internet tools instead of the tracts, pamphlets and fliers used by the colonists. It's likely that the initial Soviet coverup of the Chernobyl accident would fall apart even faster today, thanks to the interconnectedness and accessibility that the Internet provides. The stories and images we share today come at us all the time and from around the world. Think about the Iranian citizens who used their phones to document the death of a young woman named Neda during the 2009 election protests. Tunisians used social media to help oust a dictatorial president in 2011, prompting revolutions that spread across the Arab world from Egypt to Bahrain and Libya. When the devastating earthquake hit Japan in March 2011, people used Facebook and Twitter to share breaking news and information about survivors and rescue efforts, and videos posted on YouTube captured the devastation of the tsunami waves as they swept away entire communities. And the speed of the Internet ensured that citizens around the world were up to date on the Fukushima nuclear power plant crisis—the worst since Chernobyl.

## ESSENTIAL VALUES OF SEEKING AND REPORTING TRUTH

If anyone can post photos or Tweet about such dramatic events as the Arab revolutions, why would someone spend time learning to become a professional journalist?

After all, grassroots journalism is vital and cannot be underestimated. But it cannot always meet the needs of societies—democratic and nondemocratic alike. Citizens do not usually have the commitment and training of professionals, and they may not always bring strong journalistic methods and standards to their efforts. This book is about those essential values and practices that have consistently guided the work of the best professional journalists through the years. These standards are still relevant at this critical time for journalism and for you. The best journalists know their work will never present a complete picture, even when they do their job well. But they know that they come closest when they adhere to time-honored standards.

Some values are obvious. Accuracy, curiosity and skepticism are all cornerstones for the discipline of journalism. Other values are not as apparent. Learn to ask good questions and get close to the stories you report; pay close attention to details that other observers might miss; prepare yourself for the unexpected, which always happens; and act as a watchdog who can give a voice to those without influence or power.

Knowing and understanding the places you write about is essential. So is knowing what's going on around the world, in Afghanistan and Zimbabwe, in Mexico and Indonesia. Be ambitious and take risks, but learn from the inevitable failures that will occur when you take chances. Take advantage of the new tools that help you do your job faster and more efficiently, but always keep in mind that technology should be a means to an end and not the end in itself.

Strive to remember the humanity of the people you write about and your own humanity as well. In addition, understand why and how you must protect your integrity. Integrity is really all you have as a journalist. If you lose it, you lose everything.

Some of these values may sound theoretical. But journalism is not theoretical, and you must put its values into practice every day and in every story you touch. These essential values have guided the careers of many outstanding journalists whose work you'll read about in these pages. Though you may not recognize all their names, all of them were committed to getting the news out honorably and professionally. They took their work to heart and tried to make the world a better place. Most of them would tell you their work was both important and fun.

If you're lucky—and if you're good—you will be able to say the same thing.

## ESSENTIAL PRACTICES

Getting information out to people quickly is what journalists have always done. But there's more to journalism than writing, reporting and taking pictures, blogging and Tweeting. Journalism is not a licensed or regulated profession like medicine or the law, but it does carry a similar sense of responsibility and obligation to a greater good that sets it apart from a simple trade. It requires a professional commitment to essential values and practices that may sound corny to some, but which have stood the test of time. The best journalists:

- Believe their job is to seek out truth and report it accurately and fairly.

- Know the truth they discover today may change tomorrow and that they must constantly reassess what they have learned.

- Ask questions about why and how something happened, and then listen carefully to the answers.

- Consider themselves professional skeptics, always looking for proof and seeking verification for what they have been told.

- Are always prepared for the unexpected, because they know from experience that plans will often go haywire and that they must be flexible and adaptable.

- Know they have done their job well when they find and tell stories about particular people, places and events that have universal meanings.

- Know that unread and unwatched stories serve no purpose, so they are always looking for new ways to intelligently engage and inform their readers and their viewers.

- Know their stories can do good as well as harm. They weigh the consequences and try to choose their words and pictures carefully.

- Aspire to tell stories that uncover injustice, right wrongs and help people live their lives better. They look out for ordinary folks whose voices are seldom heard, and they keep a watchful eye on those in power and expose their abuses.

Journalism is sometimes seen as a profession where speed is valued above all else. Great journalists do value speed, but accuracy is sacred. Details matter and the facts must be right. Great journalists acknowledge and correct their mistakes. They also do their best to call out journalists who dishonor the profession through carelessness or such willful acts as lying, plagiarizing or making things up.

The best journalists may not always be comfortable talking about it, but they also understand that what they do has a meaning bigger than the individual writers and individual photographers or their stories and their pictures. U. S. journalists value the privileges afforded by our democracy and desire to give something in return. Whether or not they have read the work of scholar James Carey, they are likely to believe as he did, that journalism is the conversation of democracy and that one cannot exist without the other.[3] They know that a free society cannot survive if its people are not well informed. Whether they are freelancers or staff members of large companies, the best journalists are loyal to the citizens.

## ESSENTIAL PASSION FOR JOURNALISM

**N**ews organizations are in crisis, which means this is a critical time for journalism and, by extension, for democracy. Nationwide, newspaper circulation continues to plummet, news magazines are dying, and network and cable news audiences are increasingly fragmented. Advertising revenue is dropping, and thousands of journalists have lost their jobs in recent years. Traditional news organizations are looking to the Internet to protect their franchises, but no one has quite figured out which business models will work in the twenty-first century. Some journalistic entrepreneurs have capitalized in brilliant ways on new media opportunities, including the creators of the national nonprofit investigative enterprise ProPublica and those behind online news services such as *MinnPost*, the *St. Louis Beacon* and the *Rocky Mountain Investigative News Network*. The immediate future for many traditional news organizations is uncertain, and many are already history. It is not clear who will produce quality journalism and who will pay for it if the current models collapse.

Despite the gloom, the passion for journalism still lives in many of its practitioners. For journalism to survive we need journalists who understand its importance to society, believe in and are committed to its core values, and can put those values into action. We need journalists who see their jobs as more than just a way to earn a paycheck, no matter the format, structure or medium of their organization.

We need journalists who see their work as a mission, a calling. We need journalists who believe they can make a difference when they answer that call, who believe that they can help make things better for the people they write about and the people they write for.

Most importantly, we need committed journalists like you to put these values into practice to produce the kind of work that will inform and enrich society in the coming decades.

## ABOUT THIS BOOK

**T**his book includes tips and assignments to help you develop strong values and good practices that will make you a better journalist. This is not a traditional textbook that outlines how to organize, structure and write stories. There are many fine books you can turn to for that purpose. Nor is this book an overarching examination or critique of the media; it's about the distinct roles and responsibilities that set journalism apart from other media.

This book is not an elegy for newspapers either. The traditional journalistic values of newspapers remain essential today; in fact, they may be needed now more than ever. But journalism has always been about more than ink and paper. The values and practices discussed in this book apply to all forms of journalism—traditional print and broadcast as well as digital formats and formats that have yet to be conceived. Some of the values and attitudes may seem old-fashioned to you, but that doesn't mean they are outdated. They continue to apply to a journalism that is alive and essential today, and they are what journalism needs to remain vital and important to American society and to the world in the future.

For all the problems journalism faces today, for all the excesses and mistakes that have been committed by its practitioners over the years, societies continue to depend on journalists to tell them what's important and what's interesting. Events happen fast in the world and not all journalists take the time to explain what they mean. Committed journalists help their fellow citizens make sense of what's going on. The work is not easy, and it is often a thankless task. But it must be done, and done well. This book will help you develop values and practices that will guide you in your professional career.

---

### A note on the quotes and examples in this book

As a beginning journalist, you can learn from the great practitioners who have gone before you. Many of journalism's important values also apply to the arts and sciences, sports, poetry and fiction. Listen to knowledgeable individuals from those fields as well. Albert Einstein can serve as your model for the curious mind. Learn about skepticism and the danger of the obvious fact from Sherlock Holmes. Coaches and athletes can instruct you about the importance of practice and of paying attention to small details. Poets can inspire you to appreciate the diversity and the mystery of the world around you.

The best journalists embrace, and learn from, the world outside the newsroom. You should, too.

---

## CONCLUSION

 hy did Igor Kostin keep returning to Chernobyl? "The whole world was talking about the catastrophe," he explained, "and something had to be found out about it. What was I supposed to do—stay in Kiev, write a satire, drink coffee, and do nothing? How could I have? It was my job to go there, and I did my job."

This book is dedicated to the journalists past and present who hurried to the scene and did their job thoughtfully and carefully, sometimes at great personal risk. May you learn from their good work, and may you set a good example for the generation of journalists who will follow you.

## assignments

1. As a student you probably have thought about *what* you want to do as a journalist. But you might not have given as much thought to *why* you want to be a journalist. Now is a time to do that. List reasons that you want to become a journalist. Think in broad terms about the responsibilities and obligations journalists have in this country, and how their work is considered by many to be a service to our society. Think also about the important stories that journalists have reported over the years and what those stories have meant to the public. How would you want your work to be remembered at the end of your career? Save your list and add ideas to it as you read further.

2. Consider sharing some of your reasons with classmates or other journalists you know. Do they share the same reasons as you do? Discuss why or why not.

## notes

1. Elaine Steinbeck and Robert Wallsten, eds. *Steinbeck: A Life in Letters* (Penguin Books, 1976), 526.

2. Information and quotes about Igor Kostin's experiences at Chernobyl are from his book *Chernobyl: Confessions of a Reporter* (Umbrage Editions, 2006) and from an interview with *Eurozine* (April 2006). Accessed March 23, 2011, www.eurozine.com/articles/2006-04-21-kostin-en.html.

3. James Carey, "A Republic If You Can Keep It," in *James Carey: A Critical Reader,* ed. Eve Stryker Munson and Catherine A. Warren (University of Minnesota Press, 1997), 207–227.

The important thing is not to stop questioning. Curiosity has its own reason for existing. One cannot help but be in awe when he contemplates the mysteries of eternity, of life, of the marvelous structure of reality. It is enough if one tries merely to comprehend a little of this mystery every day. Never lose a holy curiosity.

ALBERT EINSTEIN[1]

# stay curious

By some standards, Roanoke, Virginia, appeared racially moderate, even progressive. African-American residents made up more than twenty percent of the population. They held elected seats on city council and appointed positions on the school board. The superintendent of schools and the police chief were both African American. For almost two decades, the city's popular mayor had been a black Republican.

Yet racial tensions persisted. The city was widely reported to be one of the most segregated in the country. Black citizens routinely voiced a distrust of city government, police, courts and schools. The distrust was also directed toward *The Roanoke Times,* which for many years ignored almost everything that happened in black neighborhoods except crime.

Reporter Mary Bishop was curious. What was the root cause of the African-American community's suspicion, she wondered, and why was it so deep? Bishop had been a member of *The Philadelphia Inquirer* team that won the Pulitzer Prize for coverage of the accident at the Three Mile Island nuclear power plant. A disciple of legendary editor Gene Roberts, Bishop could have remained at the *Inquirer,* one of the country's top newspapers, but instead she returned to her native Virginia and joined the *Times.* Soon she was a Pulitzer finalist for a

9

series about how Virginia inadequately regulated its pest control industry, a failure that led to major consumer fraud, illness, and even death for some citizens. The next year, she was a Pulitzer finalist again as a member of a team that covered a year-long miners' strike.[2]

The class and racial issues that separated Roanoke's white and black communities fascinated Bishop, and she began to write stories about what created the tensions. She developed contacts, then sources, then relationships with black citizens, many of whom had never talked to a reporter, much less a white one like Bishop.

She took a keen interest in Gainsboro, a predominantly black neighborhood that was the oldest in the city. Gainsboro had once been part of a larger, more cohesive African-American community. In the 1950s, though, the other black neighborhoods were wiped out by urban renewal, a post-war movement that swept away the parts of the nation's cities that were considered blighted slums. Like in other cities, the communities in Roanoke that were most affected were predominantly black. For many of these residents, urban renewal was a euphemism for "Negro removal."

White government officials and city leaders in Roanoke, including journalists who covered the story and wrote editorials, considered urban renewal a progressive way to clear slums and open up land for highways, industries and other civic institutions. Hearings were held and votes cast. Homes and businesses were torn down and families were forced to move, many into newly constructed public housing complexes.

*The Roanoke Times* covered the hearings in those years and informed their readers how their tax dollars were being spent. The newspaper celebrated groundbreakings for roads, businesses and a new civic center. But it did not cover the people who were forced from their homes and neighborhoods. Its journalists failed to write about those who had been displaced or acknowledge what they had lost. Like many newspapers of the time, its reporters covered issues from the perspective of those in power, namely from a biased, white perspective. The paper's coverage of urban renewal missed the most human and heartbreaking part of the story.

Mary Bishop's curiosity changed that.

For nearly three years, Bishop worked on the Gainsboro story while juggling her day-to-day reporting responsibilities. Using city directories from the 1940s and 1950s, she identified virtually every home and business seized under the urban renewal initiative and tracked down individuals who had lived or worked in those places. She documented what happened to neighborhoods and the institutions that no longer existed, digging deeper into the story to reveal the lasting effects on the families whose lives had been altered forever.

She reported her findings in a 12-page special section. It was an account of life in Roanoke that did not exist in history books, newspaper archives or in any official record. The facts were staggering.

In predominantly black Northeast Roanoke, 980 homes, 14 churches, two schools and 64 small businesses were razed. The city burned more than 100 homes because it was the cheapest way to get rid of them. "It was like looking at a war movie," the Rev. Ivory Morton, who was a child during the urban renewal years, told Bishop.

Charles Meadows recounted how he had worked for the railroad and bought a home where he and his wife raised five children. When the city forced him out, it paid him $7,800 and gave him another $2,500 to help with the move. By 1995, his old property was owned by the gas company and was part of a tract assessed at $2 million.

Bishop's persistence drew praise from white readers who were astonished at the history lesson and from black readers grateful that their story had finally been told.

What made Bishop a good reporter? No doubt it was a blend of talent, discipline and sound training from the Columbia School of Journalism plus years of experience. But another key to her success was revealed by a quote posted on the bulletin board beside her desk. The words are those of Albert Einstein: *Never lose a holy curiosity.*

Bishop always talked about the world with surprise and delight, and she encouraged her colleagues to regard their beats and the world around them with the same awe and questioning attitude with which Einstein viewed the universe. Go deeper, go higher, go farther, Bishop implored those around her. Look beneath the surface; look beyond the horizon. See what's there.

The best journalists possess an insatiable curiosity about what's going on in the world. They know people are complex and that their stories can be complicated. They know that while facts are sometimes easy to come by, the truth is often more difficult to find.

Ask yourself these questions:

- Do you seek answers to questions that others don't even think of asking?
- How willing are you to look for facts and details that others don't see or don't care about?
- Does what you don't know nag at you? How dedicated are you to asking *why* and *how* to fill in those gaps?
- How curious are you?

The answers to many of your questions will not be found on the surface, through quick interviews or perfunctory examinations of records or documents. Instead, you will have to go through longer searches, digging to find the facts and details that will make your stories come alive. The more you dig for answers, the better journalist you will become.

## CURIOSITY IS ESSENTIAL

**A**sk yourself one more question: Why would you want to be a journalist if you're not curious about the world? Curiosity is a defining trait—maybe the defining trait—of good journalists. If you don't have it, you probably should find another profession.

Curiosity, says journalism educator Mindy McAdams, is essential to becoming a good journalist. Too many students, she says, approach assignments as a burden, something they really don't want to write about. Students should recognize the honor and the responsibility they have as journalists.

"It's a great privilege to be paid for telling stories to the world," she says. "To earn that privilege, you've got to approach every opportunity to learn a new story with an open mind and a desire to find out something new. You'll never tell a great story if your strategy is to fill in blanks on a form and then simply write it up."[3]

Nigel Jaquiss won the 2005 Pulitzer for investigative reporting at the *Willamette Week* in Portland, Oregon, for stories exposing a former governor's long concealed sexual misconduct with a 14-year-old girl. Jaquiss loves that he gets paid to exercise his curiosity and learn things that no one else knows. "The rewards are inestimable," he says. "You get to go ask questions today. You get to go deep in the bowels of the library and look things up."[4]

Leon Dash, a Pulitzer Prize winner at *The Washington Post,* says his "insatiable curiosity" about people led him to in-depth exploration of such sensitive and emotional subjects as adolescent pregnancy and one family's descent into poverty, crime and drug abuse.[5] At the University of Illinois, he tries to make his students see how important it is to go beyond the standard practices of journalism to find out things they never suspected or imagined. Dash politely calls these discoveries "epiphanies." In newsrooms, they are described as "holy s---" moments in which someone uncovers something completely unanticipated.

## NURTURING CURIOSITY

**Y**ou can develop methods to nurture your curiosity. For Mary Bishop, curiosity means letting her imagination run wild, wondering about people, places and things.

Bishop credits Gene Roberts for inspiring her generation of journalists to follow their curiosity wherever it leads them. Roberts gave his reporters and editors at the *Inquirer* license to chase down the answers they needed; they felt entitled, Bishop says, to "find out anything they wanted to know."

For Roberts, curiosity and the willingness to dig for answers are the basis for the most important kind of journalism. The finest reporting, he said, always "digs, and digs, and digs. And the finest writing . . . puts things so vividly, so compellingly, that readers can see and understand and comprehend."[6]

Bishop was not afraid to dig deep or tackle a complex subject. The more complicated the subject, the more her adrenalin flowed. And the more her curiosity kicked into overdrive, and the harder she worked.

Sometimes Bishop was curious about what was happening at a particular moment, but often her curiosity was about events in the past, why they had taken place, and what they meant for the present. The only way to uncover the meaning from the past was to keep digging like a good archaeologist.

"Why is it this way?" she asked herself about Roanoke's racial history. "Why did they set up the town this way? And then it's imagining yourself in another person's shoes, thinking about what their point of view is, how they grew up."

New reporters often have a hard time understanding the importance of curiosity, and how lack of it can drain a story of vitality. Think for a moment about a story you've recently completed, and then answer these questions as honestly as possible:

- How genuinely interested were you about the person or the issue that you were writing about?
- Did you approach the story with an open but questioning attitude, or did you accept what you were told at face value?
- What do you now wish you had asked about, or what do you wish you had challenged?
- What do you wish you had learned but didn't?

Most likely you could have asked additional questions in those moments when you wanted to get a quote and move on. Curiosity means keeping your mind and your eyes open and willingly asking another round of *why* questions. Now that you're aware of how you approached your last story, here are some ways to foster your curiosity for the next one.

## Take note

Dan Barry, who writes the "This Land" column for *The New York Times,* says he keeps thoughts and notes about things that arouse his curiosity: "Where are the Munchkins today? Who gets to be judge at a county fair baking contest, and does the power go to the judges' head? What are the auditions like for the Mormon Tabernacle Choir?"[7] Carry a notebook to jot down your questions or use a voice recording program on your mobile phone to note something that piques your curiosity.

Sometimes, Barry says, these questions lead to weightier issues. What is it like to witness an execution? What do you do when the Mississippi River threatens to flood your town?

## Ask why and how

The best journalists—the ones who are most curious about the world—understand how difficult it is to dig for answers to complex questions. The work is equally hard for geniuses such as Einstein and for experienced journalists to write honestly and deeply about what is going on around them. As a beginning journalist, it will be hard for you too, but you must never stop digging. Covering the *who, what, when* and *where* of an event is easy. Your job is to get beyond that and explain *why* and *how* and to look for the reasons things are the way they are.

A *why* question led journalist and novelist Tom Wolfe to write *The Right Stuff,* his epic account of America's first astronauts. Why, he wondered, would a man be willing "to sit up on top of an enormous Roman candle, such as a Redstone, Atlas, Titan, or Saturn rocket, and wait for someone to light the fuse?"[8]

*Why* is always the best question, *Washington Post* staff writer Joel Achenbach says.

"This is not to insult those who handle what, where, when or who, nor even the masters of how," Achenbach writes in *Why Things Are.*[9] "But those questions are too often answered through pure description, the mere delivery of information, the recitation of facts, trivia, minutiae.

"When you ask why, you are shooting much higher. . . . What makes 'why' such a special question is that it is entirely human. 'Why' does not occur naturally in the universe. The universe just IS, from all appearances. . . . But if there were no people like us, there would be no asking *why* these things are."

The more experienced you become, the more naturally you will remember to ask *how* and *why.* In the meantime you may want to write those very questions or even just the word *why* at the top of every page of your reporter's notebook to remind you of their importance. Dig for those answers, and you will be rewarded.

Unbridled curiosity drives many young journalists. Christina M. Woods, who covered cultural affairs at *The Wichita Eagle,* says she was always nosy as a child. It wasn't until she got to middle school that she learned that journalists make a living by asking questions and telling others what they find out.

"Curiosity is key," she says. "I'm really into finding out people's stories, what motivates people, what drives them, what makes them the way they are."[10]

Hilary Lehman's parents are journalists, but she doubted that she would follow in their footsteps. She'd seen the stress that comes with the job, and she knew the hours were long and the pay not great. She went to the University of Florida thinking about science or math as a major. In those classes, though, she found herself in boring routines, not able to ask questions or interact with people as she'd learned to do at dinner table discussions with her parents.

"Journalism was the thing I thought I'd never do," she said. "But it fit my personality. I could be myself. I enjoy writing, but more than that I am a nosy person. I like to know what's going on."[11]

She changed her major to journalism and went to work for the *Independent Florida Alligator,* the university's student newspaper. She wanted to find out about people, and journalism gave her the opportunity to do just that.

"You can just go up to a person on the street," she said. "Journalism gives you an excuse to ask them anything."

That's the great thing about being a journalist, Lehman's mother told her one time as she worked on a story. You get to satisfy your curiosity.

## CONCLUSION

Mary Bishop retired from the newspaper business in 2002. But her influence lives on.

She received a lot of recognition during her career, but journalism for her was not about awards or personal honor. It was about integrity, compassion for others and her passionate belief that journalism makes a difference. She always knew that the most important stories were about people, and she was unflinchingly honest in telling those stories, both about the rich and the powerful and especially about the poor and the weak.

Of all the stories she wrote over more than three decades as a reporter, she remains most proud of investigating the effect of urban renewal on Roanoke's black community. It was a story that had been around for more than forty years, she says, and yet no one had done the digging to uncover it.

"It was a chance to tell a story that no one had told," she says. "It happened under everyone's watch, so slowly. No one thought about it because the people were so devalued."

Unfortunately, journalists today work in newsroom environments that do not always provide the time or the incentives necessary to satisfy our curiosity about what's going on around us. The news world is 24/7. When something happens, just about everyone knows right away. Then we move on to the next breaking news event, and we must be the first to tell our readers and viewers what is happening.

Like every journalist, you will learn the excitement of a breaking story and the thrill that comes with being the first to tell it. (Part of the definition of news is, after all, that it is *new*.) But you need to be more than a stenographer who records what happens or a transcriber who merely writes down what people say.

Maintain the passionate curiosity that drives your journalistic ventures. Explore the questions that arise and don't be satisfied with scratching the surface.

*Never lose a holy curiosity.* Einstein's words deserve a place on bulletin boards in every newsroom in the country. Put them above your desk, put them in your notes, and live by them.

## checklist

- **Keep a journal.** Take notes about what you see, hear and experience, and not just for the stories you're reporting. What doesn't add up or make sense? What insights and questions do you take away from your daily experiences?

- **Talk to people and listen to what they tell you.** Be curious, even politely nosy. Why did someone do something a particular way?

What were her motivations? What are the things she says that are surprising, even astonishing? Record what you learn.

- **Read.** Go through magazines, books, newspapers, websites. Don't just read the ones you agree with or that cover topics that you're most interested in. Investigate diverse subjects you've never studied. Record your thoughts and observations.

- **Be a student forever.** If you're still in school, you may be looking forward to the day you finally graduate from college. But don't stop learning. Continue to take classes when you can to discover new things about art or literature, learn a new language, or take up a new sport.

- **Be open-minded.** Prematurely making up your mind up about a subject will kill your curiosity. Some things you're certain about are bound to be wrong, so be willing to change your mind.

## assignments

1. Remember as a child always asking your parents, *What's that?* and *Why?* This natural curiosity may have been so extreme that perhaps your parents or teachers told you to be quiet. You probably didn't stay quiet for long. You had to tell someone what you had learned or discovered.

   Approach your next story with the curiosity and naïveté of a child. Even if you've covered the subject before, put aside your assumptions and approach it anew. Draw up a list of as many basic questions you can think of, and use them to go after the story:
   - *What's that?*
   - *Why are things this way?*
   - *Why aren't things different?*
   - *Who's responsible?*
   - *What's going to happen next?*
   - *Where else can I go for information?*
   - *Who should I talk to next?*

2. When you've finished your reporting, study what you've learned. What are the epiphanies that you've had? What surprises have you uncovered? What have you discovered that you—and maybe no one else—knew or imagined?

3. Finally, analyze your approach to the story. What have you learned about your own sense of curiosity? What will do differently next time?

## notes

1. Albert Einstein to William Miller, quoted in *Life Magazine,* May 2, 1955.

2. Interview with Mary Bishop, August 31, 2008. Her story "Street By Street, Block By Block: How Urban Renewal Uprooted Black Roanoke," ran in the January 29, 1995, edition of *The Roanoke Times.*

3. Mindy McAdams, *Teaching Online Journalism* blog post, September 25, 2007. Accessed March 23, 2011, from http://mindymcadams.com/tojou/2007/advice-for-journalism-students/.

4. Interview with Nigel Jaquiss, February 15, 2009.

5. Interview with Leon Dash, January 27, 2009.

6. Gene Roberts, *IRE Journal* (winter 1988). Quotes reprinted from Roberts's November 1987 speech as part of the Otis Chandler Lecture Series at the University of Southern California.

7. Dan Barry, "Talk to the Newsroom: 'This Land' Columnist." New York Times Online, February 19, 2009. Accessed March 23, 2011, from www.nytimes.com/2009/02/16/business/media/16askthetimes.html.

8. Tom Wolfe, introduction to *The Right Stuff* (Farrar, Strauss, 1983).

9. Joel Achenbach, introduction to *Why Things Are: Answers to Every Essential Question in Life* (Ballantine Books, 1991).

10. Interview with Christina Woods, January 9, 2009.

11. Interview with Hilary Lehman, February 2, 2009.

## CHAPTER 3

There is nothing more deceptive than an obvious fact.

SHERLOCK HOLMES,
THE BOSCOMBE VALLEY MYSTERY

# get it right

The first bulletin moved shortly after 2 p.m. one late summer day: U. S. Rep. Stephanie Tubbs Jones of Ohio had suffered a brain hemorrhage while driving in suburban Cleveland the night before and had died. *The Washington Post*'s Capitol Briefing blog reported her death at 2:10 p.m. Twenty minutes later, the Associated Press moved a one-sentence NewsAlert from Washington, attributing the information to a Democratic Party official. *The Cleveland Plain Dealer* soon posted a story on its website, citing anonymous sources. CNN, CBS News and Fox News also moved stories saying that Tubbs Jones was dead.[1]

Tubbs Jones had been the first African-American woman elected to Congress from Ohio, and she had achieved prominence during her five terms in office. There was only one problem with the bulletins. Tubbs Jones was still alive, though in critical condition. She did not die until four hours after her death was first reported.

The news organizations scrambled to correct their mistake and then to explain how they screwed up an important story. The *Post* said its report was based on a reliable Democratic source and other news outlets. The *Plain Dealer* said it had multiple trusted sources in Cleveland and Washington, including a high-ranking congressional source. The AP said a Democratic Party official confirmed Tubbs Jones' death on condition of anonymity.

Those accounts were merely explanations. They couldn't excuse the fact that the news organizations had violated the first rule of journalism: Get it right.

Journalists make mistakes. In the rush to get the news out first, reporters and their editors may rely on a single source who may not be ideal. They don't take the time to confirm the information and double-check the details they've been given. They're in such a hurry they ignore signals that indicate something is wrong.

Other times, the deadline is not to blame. Things seem obvious: assumptions are made, hazy memories are recalled, and outdated or erroneous stories are consulted. A reporter fails to verify the spelling of a name or check an address. Another reporter adds numbers incorrectly or simply doesn't know how to calculate percentages. Errors creep into the stories and the damage is done.

Unless you lived in Ohio or Washington, D. C., or were paying particularly close attention to the news that afternoon in August 2008, you might have missed the faulty reporting of Tubbs Jones' death. Most Americans either didn't notice or quickly forgot the mistake, which was an online error that was corrected quickly. The news organizations that reported Tubbs Jones' death prematurely are all respected, hard-working and committed to fast and accurate reporting. They believed their sources to be reliable, and they saw other journalists reporting the congresswoman's death as a fact. Who could fault them for wanting to get the story out as fast as possible?

The quest for speed led to shortcuts, which led to sloppiness and a collective failure that created a dangerous downward spiral. New reports were based on the preceding erroneous ones. None of the news organizations did what they should have done at the beginning: talk to the hospital or Tubbs Jones' office or family to find out what had really happened. A simple phone call might have stopped the wrong story before it ever started. Online corrections could not erase the fact that a serious mistake had been made.

Even if you didn't know about the Tubbs Jones story, you may be familiar with these journalistic goofs by other major news organizations:

- During the 2004 presidential campaign, the CBS News program *60 Minutes* reported the existence of memos that raised serious questions about George W. Bush's service in the National Guard. CBS never confirmed the authenticity of the memos, and the network defended its reporting until the source of the memos admitted lying about how he had obtained them. The network finally acknowledged that the memos should not have been used without verification. Longtime anchor Dan Rather and others connected with the story eventually lost their jobs.

*Newsweek* reported that American interrogators at Guantanamo Bay had flushed a copy of the Quran, the Muslim holy text, down a toilet while questioning detainees. The report sparked anti-American protests and deadly riots in Afghanistan and other Muslim countries. *Newsweek* eventually apologized, saying its confidential source for the story was no longer sure the story was true.

*The Chicago Tribune* ran a package of stories in 2005 about federal indictments against alleged mob members on charges ranging from racketeering to murder. The story included photos of men who had been charged by the feds, including one of Frank Calabrese Sr., a mob *capo,* or street boss. The problem? The picture was of a different Frank Calabrese, a businessman with no mob ties. The following day the *Tribune* ran a front-page photo taken by a local college student of a man riding a bicycle; the paper identified the bicyclist as Joseph "the Clown" Lombardo, another indicted mobster. But the bicyclist was a 69-year-old man who had merely been out for a bike ride—not Lombardo. The *Tribune* apologized for both mistakes. Calabrese, the businessman, sued the paper for defamation.

These stories prompted news organizations to promise that corrective steps would prevent similar errors in the future. The errors and the resulting corrections were embarrassing not only for the journalists responsible for the mistakes, but also for the profession of journalism as a whole.

## EVERY STORY IS IMPORTANT

Most mistakes made by journalists are less spectacular. Look at page 2 of most newspapers and you'll see more common errors. A student's age is incorrect in a story about a school play. The last name of a man killed in a car wreck is misspelled. A review of a new movie says it is playing somewhere it isn't. A business story about a restaurant opening misreports its hours of operation.

Taken individually, these journalistic errors may seem trivial or sometimes even amusing. A July 2, 2008, *Wall Street Journal* correction noted that a review of the DVD release of "Silent Running" erroneously stated that the androids in the 1972 science fiction movie were played by dwarfs when in fact they had been played by bilateral amputees. Journalists make a big mistake, though, if they consider an error either amusing or trivial. All the mistakes in our stories hurt us. Journalists are judged first and foremost on their commitment to accuracy. If we don't verify the details of our stories—even the tiniest ones—readers and viewers will notice and begin to question everything we do.

In fact, they are already suspicious. A 2009 survey by the Pew Research Center for the People and the Press found the public's perception of the accuracy of news stories at its lowest point in more than two decades. A Gallup Poll the same year showed that only about 45 percent of Americans had confidence in the media to report the news fully, accurately and fairly. If readers and viewers believe journalists are careless, inaccurate and unreliable, they will turn to us less often. Eventually, they'll search for alternative sources of news and information they can trust, leaving us without an audience.

No story is too small for detailed accuracy. Strive for the same standards of accuracy, fairness and honesty no matter what your story. Every story is important to someone, and all should be important to you because each story pursued accurately and fairly will enhance your credibility. Each story reported carelessly will undermine it.

Get it right. It sounds so simple. Yet as journalists have discovered, getting things right is neither easy nor fast. The difficult aspect of your job is not the writing or the interviewing; it is making sure that everything is correct. As a journalist, your passion for accuracy must be obsessive. Develop reporting habits that help you verify your stories and document their accuracy. Without the commitment and dedication to getting things right, nothing you do will matter.

## Common errors

| | |
|---|---|
| Misquotes | Typos and general misspellings |
| Incorrect headlines | Incorrect job titles |
| Numerical errors | Misspelled names |

*Source:* Craig Silverman, author of *Regret the Error.*[2]

## AVOIDING MISTAKES

Journalists make mistakes for many reasons. Consider these:

- A reporter forgets to double-check a spelling or a math calculation. His haste to be first with a story may conflict with his obligation to get things right. The pressure to get a story online quickly makes it even more difficult to ensure that accuracy remains our primary concern.

- A reporter and her source may not communicate clearly. What the source means is not what the reporter hears.

- A source gives a reporter erroneous information. The source may be simply misinformed, or he may have ulterior or even sinister motives. Either way, the error is published.

- An editor changes something in a story and makes it wrong. Editors may make assumptions about stories and fail to ask questions that would prevent the introduction of errors where none existed before.

Explanations for journalistic mistakes are countless. Ultimately, though, you're responsible for any errors in your published story. You can explain them, but don't make excuses for them. Chapter 4 talks more about this responsibility. Once you are aware of how easily mistakes happen, take steps to do things right. A good place to start is with your sources.

### Develop your sources

Developing strong and trusting relationships with sources is essential. They can give you information and lead you to documents and records that provide authority for your stories. Get to know your sources before you need them, and they need to get to know you, too, on a professional level and, to a certain extent, a personal level as well. Trust can only be established over time. Your sources will come to trust you after you've developed a relationship with them and demonstrated your commitment to accuracy and fairness.

Second-hand sources are not always reliable, so look for individuals with first-hand knowledge or experience about your stories. The people who claimed that Stephanie Tubbs Jones had died were not in touch with the hospital or her family. You need to talk to people who know the facts, not those who think they know. If a source isn't certain about what she's telling you, ask whom you can talk to or where you can go to find the hard facts. Seek information that can be proved and verified.

Then cite your sources. Attribution builds authority. Be transparent and let your audience know where you got your information. Provide links to online documents, records and other web-based references so readers can see your sources for themselves. Avoid anonymous sources; readers and viewers distrust them. Use them only when the information they provide is essential to the story and you can find no on-the-record source. Make sure you've exhausted all other options and you've discussed the circumstances thoroughly with your editor.

Check with your sources after the story is published or broadcast. If you're honest and direct with them beforehand, you have nothing to fear from their reaction afterward to a story that is accurate, fair and honest. They may point you in a new direction for a follow-up or your next story.

### Pay attention to small details

Successful people in any profession know that attention to detail is a key ingredient to achieving success. Consider UCLA basketball coach John Wooden. From the mid-1960s until his retirement in 1974, Wooden won 10 national championships over 12 seasons, including seven in a row. His teams had an 88-game winning streak, recorded four 30–0 seasons, and won a record 38 straight NCAA tournament games.[3]

Wooden insisted his players pay attention to small things. Wooden knew that no matter how talented his players were, they needed to understand the basics of the game. The first day of practice each year, Wooden demonstrated to his rookies and veterans how to work their socks around their toes, their heels and then their ankles, snugly and smoothly to prevent blisters. Then he demonstrated how to lace and tie their shoes so they would not come untied and trip them up during practice or a game.

Only after they had learned the importance of the little things did he take them onto the court and allow them to practice basketball. Just as Wooden's players learned the right way to put on their socks and shoes, you must learn that accuracy is the foundation for everything you do as a reporter. If you don't get things right from the start, you'll trip yourself up as a journalist. Hone your skills by following these tips:

- **Double-check all the names and numbers in your stories.** If you record your interviews, ask individuals to spell their names and then repeat the spelling to them for verification. When interviewing someone in person, show her how you've written down her name and ask her to verify its accuracy. Read back addresses and phone numbers, too. Call phone numbers to double-check their accuracy if you include them in your story. Check URLs by typing them into a browser.

- **Learn basic math.** Check your numbers. Learn how to calculate percentages. Don't make your audience add, subtract, multiply or divide. Do it for them and then double-check your answers.

- **Get a response.** Don't tell your readers that someone couldn't be reached for comment. Be a reporter. Track down the person and talk to her. If she won't answer your questions, at least let your readers know that you've asked the questions.

- **Ask straightforward questions.** Be clear. Don't be devious, back-handed or indirect.

- **Don't assume you know the answers to your questions.** Listen—really listen—to what you are told. Don't assume you understand the answer you've been given. Ask another question. Don't assume the information you have been given is correct. Check it, then check it again.

- **Don't rely on your memory.** You won't remember everything you've seen and heard. Your memory will become even less reliable as you get older. Look up documents and records and talk to sources who know the details.

- **Don't quote other news stories.** Use other news sources for tips, not as primary sources. If another reporter has a fact or detail in her story, do not assume it's correct. Go to the source and confirm the information first-hand. The source may have learned something new, or may have changed her thinking about the issue.

- **Don't trust story archives.** The story that someone else wrote or produced may be wrong. Don't repeat an error. Check things out again.

## Be careful to the very end

When you've finished your draft, verify the facts in your story against your notes and other source material. Use independent, authoritative sources. If you find a discrepancy, go back to the original source and clear it up. Always ask if your reporting supports each assertion in your story. Be sure you can verify what you've written.

Print out your story and read it thoroughly before you turn it in. You may be surprised at what you missed on the computer screen. Verify your words and your numbers. If something doesn't sound or

## Examples of getting it right

Talk to good reporters and you'll discover what they do to get things right.

When Laura Frank was a journalist with the *Rocky Mountain News,* she filled three-ring binders with key documents for her stories about a U. S. Department of Labor program that denied compensation to former nuclear-arms workers sickened by exposure to radiation. Frank carefully labeled each document, showing when she obtained it and what it included. Her detailed organization was essential because of the delicate nature of her stories and because a hostile Labor Department refused to cooperate during her investigation. But their efforts to poke holes in her work fell flat. The only mistake the Labor Department found was a single graphic that included a departmental seal, which suggested that it was an official government graphic when it was not.[4]

*New York Times* projects reporter Ron Nixon learned the importance of accuracy from his first editor, Zack Weston, who owned a string of African-American community newspapers in Nixon's home state of South Carolina. Weston taught Nixon how to obtain documents and records, and he wouldn't tolerate mistakes. Nixon says he can drive colleagues crazy when they're working on a project. Sensitive stories are footnoted to document the origin of every piece of information. Files are carefully organized, and every fact and detail is cross-checked.[5]

Christina M. Woods discovered that she had to be particularly careful when writing about sensitive topics such as immigration and race relations for *The Wichita Eagle,* her hometown newspaper. At first she routinely read quotes back to people she interviewed to make sure that they were accurate and in context. Then she began e-mailing the quotes to sources. She not only got the same assurances of accuracy, but she also created a paper trail that documented her diligence.[6]

Kerry DeRochi described for her colleagues at *The Virginian-Pilot* the method she learned when she was a *Newsweek* intern. She would print out her stories and go through them line by line, word by word with a red marker, verifying each fact against her notes or another source or reference material. It was a time-consuming pain, she said, but it worked.[7]

feel right, stop and check it out. Resolve what's bothering you. If in doubt, leave it out. It's better to omit a questionable detail than to publish or broadcast something that is wrong.

Don't fall into the trap of assuming you know what's correct. Instead, ask yourself questions such as, *Was that exactly what he said?* Then check your notes and recordings. If it isn't exact, do not use it as a direct quote. *Was that exactly what she meant?* If you paraphrase, accurately convey the meaning as well as the context. *What brand of beer was on the table when the shooting started?* Details matter. Blue Moon is not the same as Blue Ribbon. *Was the murder victim wearing a scarf or a shawl?* Be precise. A scarf and a shawl are similar but not the same. Which is correct, *Condoleeza* or *Condoleezza* Rice? One is right and the other is not.

Never forget the far-reaching consequences of a journalist's mistakes. If one story contains inaccuracies, readers will suspect your other stories are wrong as well. If one reporter is careless, readers and viewers will come to believe that other journalists at the organization are just as sloppy. A reporter who makes mistakes tarnishes his own reputation as well as that of colleagues, his news organization, and his profession. Many readers already believe the worst about journalists. Don't give them any reasons to question your integrity and commitment to getting things right.

Even when your audience disagrees with a story—your topic may be something the audience finds objectionable or be about an issue with which they disagree—they expect the basic facts to be accurate. They will notice if they are not, they will not forget, and they often will not forgive. When they see a detail that they know is not right, they will begin to doubt the other things that you report. "If he couldn't spell the name correctly, what else did he get wrong?"

## CONCLUSION

The mistakes surrounding the 2008 death of Stephanie Tubbs Jones should have taught journalists a lesson. Unfortunately, not everyone learned it.

A gunman opened fire at a public gathering held by Congresswoman Gabrielle Giffords for constituents on January 8, 2011, in Tucson, Arizona. The scene was one of pandemonium, but it was clear many people were seriously injured. Because it was Saturday, many news organizations were lightly staffed. Reporters around the country scrambled to learn the scope of the attacks and the fate of Rep. Giffords. Relying on eyewitnesses and governmental sources, NPR first reported online that Giffords had been killed. CNN followed with a similar online report. Fox News and *The New York Times* did the same. Other organizations cited the first reports and repeated the story.

Six people were killed that day in Tucson, but Giffords wasn't one of them. The news organizations quickly retracted their stories and acknowledged their mistakes. Once again, journalists examined what had gone wrong and why.

"There should be no room for doubt when a news organization declares someone dead," said Scott Simon, the host of NPR's "Weekend Edition Saturday" and a friend of Giffords and her husband. "They should wait until the medical authorities directly involved declare death, or close family members announce it."[8]

As a beginning journalist, you must learn the lesson of what happened with Stephanie Tubbs Jones and Gabrielle Giffords.

Accuracy is what counts in journalism; almost right is still wrong. Being first doesn't matter if you're wrong.

Commit yourself to accuracy in everything you write, produce and edit. If you fail in that basic commitment, you will lose, and the communities that you profess to serve will lose, too. So will your colleagues, the news organizations you work for and the craft of journalism.

## checklist

- **Aim for what is provably true, not what is probably true.** Your job is to verify the details in your story. Something may sound good, but don't report it if you can't prove it.

- **Double-check all your facts, especially names and numbers.** Names and numbers trip up even the most experienced reporters. Check spellings and make sure you don't use someone's first name when you mean to use his surname. Use a calculator to ensure that your math is correct.

- **Never assume.** If you assume something is right you may fail to check it out. Always verify, whether your source is in-person, in a document or online.

- **Do not rely on your memory, archives or other news stories.** Your memory may play tricks on you. Old stories may contain errors that were never corrected.

- **Develop sources with first-hand knowledge about your story and find records and documents that support it. Cite your sources.** Journalists writing about Reps. Tubbs Jones and Giffords relied on sources who didn't have first-hand information about their conditions. You build authority when you use and cite official documents and records.

- Read a hard copy of your story carefully one last time before you turn it in. You'll catch errors you missed on your screen.

- Listen to your gut. If something doesn't sound or feel right, check it out. If you're not certain it's correct, leave it out.

- Check back with your sources after your story runs. They'll appreciate it. Plus they'll let you know what you got right and— more importantly—if you got something wrong.

## assignments

Print out your next story and proofread it, completing these tasks:

1. First, mark each fact in the story, including names, dates, address-es, numbers, direct quotes, information taken from documents, details that you may have seen or heard directly and details that have come from other human sources.

2. Line by line and word by word, verify each fact against your notes, documents and reference materials. Highlight in yellow any facts or details that do not match your notes or other source materials.

3. Double-check all the information that you could not verify and get it right. Turn in the story only when you're certain every-thing is correct.

## notes

1. Information about the reporting of Stephanie Tubbs Jones' death comes from Meghan Barr, "Stephanie Tubbs Jones, Passionate Politician, Dies at 58," Associated Press, August 20, 2008; Stephen Koff and Sabrina Eaton, *The Plain Dealer,* August 20, 2008; and Greg Mitchell, "News Outlets Report Death of Con-gresswoman—When Still Alive," *Editor & Publisher,* August 20, 2008.

2. Craig Silverman, *Regret the Error: How Media Mistakes Pollute the Press and Imperil Free Speech* (Union Square Press, 2007).

3. Lessons taught by Wooden can be found in John Wooden and Steve Jamison, *The Essential Wooden* (McGraw-Hill, 2007); *The*

*UCLA Dynasty* (HBO Films, 2007); and *Newsweek,* October 25, 1999, p. 64.

4. Interview with Laura Frank, January 12, 2009.

5. Interview with Ron Nixon, December 30, 2008.

6. Interview with Christina Woods, January 9, 2009.

7. Kerry DeRochi, "How One Reporter Almost Always Gets It Right," *Continuous Information,* an in-house newsletter produced by the Norfolk *Virginian-Pilot,* September 27, 1994.

8. Scott Simon was quoted in a January 19, 2011, column by NPR ombudsman Alicia Shepard: www.npr.org/blogs/ombudsman/2011/01/19/132964802/how-npr-giffords-mistake-hurt-the-families.

# 4

A man of genius makes no mistakes. His errors are . . . the portals of discovery.

JAMES JOYCE, *ULYSSES*

# admit your mistakes

**M**aurice Possley made a mistake when he was a young reporter at Chicago's City News Bureau, which covered local and breaking news. Possley was writing a news obituary, a routine assignment except for one detail—the deceased was related to the editor of the *Chicago Daily News.* Possley made some calls and filed his story, which then went out on the bureau's wire service to news organizations across the city.

Paul Zimbrakos, the bureau's city editor, soon got a call from someone at the *Daily News.* Possley had misspelled the first name of Daryle Feldmeir, the *Daily News* editor.

"How could this happen?" Zimbrakos demanded. Possley knew what Zimbrakos really meant: How could you be so *effing* stupid?

Someone at the *Daily News* had given Possley the name over the phone. "They either gave it to me wrong, or I took it down wrong. I never double-checked it," Possley said. "All I had to do was look at the masthead of the damn newspaper."

More than a quarter of a century later, after winning one Pulitzer Prize at the *Chicago Tribune* and being a finalist for three others, Possley still remembers his horrible feeling that day.

"I was so embarrassed. We put it out on the wire and someone from the *Daily News* saw it and called up and said, 'Hey, dopey, you misspelled Feldmeir's name.' "[1]

s you learned in the previous chapter, diligence prevents mistakes. Check, double-check and even triple-check the facts in your stories. Your verification system will ensure you haven't been careless with any details.

The truth, though, is that all journalists make mistakes and you will too. The very nature of daily journalism precludes an accuracy rate of 100 percent. Nowadays, the speed demanded by online reporting creates even more dangers, but if you're serious about your craft, you'll learn from mistakes that will sear themselves into your memory.

## TAKING RESPONSIBILITY FOR YOUR MISTAKES

hat should you do when you get something wrong?

First, admit it. A published or broadcast error is visible to the entire community and, thanks to the Internet, the whole world. Readers and viewers will recognize your mistake, even if they do not call, e-mail or Tweet to tell you about it. Whether the mistake is one of commission or omission, you must accept and acknowledge your responsibility.

This all-important first step may be hard for you. No one likes to be wrong, especially about a crucial fact in your story that could damage your reputation as a journalist. Discovering a seemingly minor mistake in a story that you've labored over hits you directly in the gut. You have seen what happens to journalists who are inaccurate, and you know you can lose your job if you make too many errors. You might convince yourself the mistake wasn't really that important. Why admit a minor flaw in an otherwise strong story?

Possley says the culture of many news organizations discourages reporters from admitting mistakes. Some reporters lie about their errors or try to cover them up. Don't fall into that trap. As a principled journalist, you must admit any mistake that is called to your attention or that you learn about independently.

Admitting and correcting errors will help build your credibility and the credibility of your news organization. "The really big part of building trustworthiness. . . with your organization is being able to take responsibility for your mistakes when you make them, even the small ones, the smallest one, because they matter to someone," said Courtney Lowery, managing editor of NewWest.net, which covers the Rocky Mountain West.[2] "They matter to the person whose name you misspelled. . . . So we want to be as accurate and fair as possible, and when we're wrong we want to own up to it because that is where the trust and the relationship builds between NewWest and our readers."

## Don't make excuses

The next step is to correct your mistake. You may find public acknowledgment embarrassing. That's good. Mistakes *should* be embarrassing to journalists and their organizations. But shame or embarrassment over a mistake is much less traumatic than the dishonor that comes when mistakes go uncorrected or are covered up.

Your correction should be clear, concise and devoid of excuses. The code of ethics for the nonprofit online news organization Propublica says that mistakes must be corrected fully, quickly and ungrudgingly.[3] That should be your standard as well, whether you're writing for print, broadcast or online. Don't duck responsibility if the error was something you could and should have verified. Print and broadcast corrections should be published or aired quickly and prominently. Mistakes on Web pages should be corrected as soon as possible. In the case of significant online errors, make sure the correction states what was corrected and when.

A journalist who hides or ignores his mistakes may be able to hold onto his job for a time. Eventually, though, the errors will become so significant that stories will collapse under their weight. So will the journalist's reputation and that of his or her news organization. Accept your responsibility.

## Learn from your errors

To acknowledge and correct your mistakes is not enough. You must also learn from them, and not make the same ones again. As a beginning journalist, you may rely on an editor to correct your punctuation or massage your sentences before your story is published. You may struggle with math and depend on another editor to check the percentages for your story about an increase in tax rates.

It wasn't a rookie mistake that haunts Leon Dash. He was an established reporter at *The Washington Post,* and his investigation of the nation's prison system had been turned into a book. He had won an Overseas Press Club award for his series written during the 10 weeks he was embedded with rebel forces in Angola. While working on a series about the spread of heroin in the nation's capital, his managing editor assigned him to cover a big cocaine bust. Dash resisted, but his editor insisted.

Dash attended a press conference where details of the bust were rolled out, and his story ran on the front page. It stated that someone had snorted a gram of cocaine. Readers pointed out that a person who snorted that much coke would be dead within a couple of minutes.

The calls came from people who knew what they were talking about, namely drug users and dealers. Dash had substituted *grams* for *milligrams,* and no one caught the mistake before the story was printed. The detail seemed logical enough, except to anyone who sold or did drugs.

Dash, who won a Pulitzer Prize for explanatory journalism in 1995, was devastated by the error.

"This may not seem like a big deal to other people," he says now. "I was in too much of a hurry. . . . What hurt me so bad was that it was a simple thing that I should have checked, and I didn't check."[4]

Grow up. Your editors will backstop you for a while, but they will have no patience if you make the same kinds of errors repeatedly. They will expect you to learn proper grammar and sentence structure. They will demand that you do the math yourself, correctly. They will insist that you be accountable for your work.

Robin Toner, the first woman national political correspondent for *The New York Times,* covered five presidential elections, numerous state and federal campaigns, abortion rights battles, judicial nominations, and health care issues. When she died of colon cancer in 2008, her news obituary not only cited the high-profile stories she had covered, but more importantly it praised her passionate commitment to getting things right.[5]

Her obituary pointed out that in a craft in which little errors "are commonplace and bigger mistakes a regular occupational hazard, Ms. Toner devised a meticulous method for checking and rechecking names, dates, facts and figures in her raw copy, a step few reporters take. As a result: barely half a dozen published corrections over the years, on more than 1,900 articles with her byline."

Toner's record for accuracy was not one hundred percent, but it was about as close as any journalist can get. Apart from her stories, Toner's disciplined approach to getting things right may be her most important legacy.

## Apologize, and mean it

After you admit, correct and learn from your mistake, the last step may be the hardest. Contact persons who may have been victimized by your error. Explain honestly and forthrightly how the mistake occurred without shifting blame. Don't be shocked by angry reactions. But you may be surprised to find out how forgiving people can be if your personally, thoughtfully and honestly say *I'm sorry. I really screwed up. I hope you'll forgive me.*

Your relationship with your readers or viewers depends on your credibility, and every mistake chips away at it. Your audience will respect you more if you acknowledge your faults directly. The act of apologizing should be humbling enough to make you even more diligent in your efforts to avoid future mistakes.

## CONCLUSION

You will make mistakes in your career as a journalist. Recognizing your fallibility does not lessen your obligation to write accurate stories and to admit, correct and learn from your mistakes. Commit yourself to getting things right; if you sacrifice accuracy for speed, your credibility and reputation will deservedly crumble.

The best journalists learn from their mistakes and the mistakes of others, and they do everything they can to make sure their stories are right.

Admit your mistakes. Learn from them. And don't make the same ones again.

## checklist

Bear Bryant, the legendary University of Alabama football coach, told his players that there were only three things they could do when they messed up on the field: Admit their mistake, learn from it and don't make it again. The same principles apply to your work as a journalist.

- **Admit your mistake.** When you discover that you've made an error, don't cover it up. Confront your discomfort; it's a sign of character to take responsibility for your errors.

- **Correct your mistake.** Whether your error appeared in print, online, on radio or on television, make certain your correction runs as quickly as possible and that it clearly identifies what the mistake was. A defensive or muddled correction can be as bad as the original error.

- **Apologize for your mistake.** You may not always be able to do this in person, but you owe it to your sources and your subjects to let them know that you take errors seriously and regret them.

- **Learn from your mistake.** What caused the error? Review all the steps that led to your mistake, so you're not likely to make the same one again.

## assignments

1. In the previous chapter you analyzed your most recent story by going through a hard copy line by line with a red pen, verifying each fact against your notes or another piece of known information or reference material.

    Now ask at least one major source you interviewed to meet you in person so he or she can read the story in your presence. Ask the individual to grade you on its accuracy. Are the names, ages, dates, addresses and other personal information correct? Does your source feel he or she was quoted correctly, whether directly or indirectly? Are other details in the story correct? Did you make assumptions that were not substantiated by the facts? Does your source believe all your facts and details are placed within a proper context? Was there anything unfair or inappropriate in the story, according to your source?

2. What grade did your source give you? What kinds of errors or factual problems, if any, did your source find? Were there common issues with things that were either incorrect or not verifiable? What lessons can you learn from your mistakes? What lessons can you learn from what you did well?

## notes

1. Interview with Maurice Possley, January 24, 2009.

2. Courtney Lowery, "Accuracy and Fact-checking in Journalism." Knight Citizen News Network. Available online. www.kcnn.org/ principles/accuracy_and_fact_checking_in_journalism. Accessed March 24, 2011.

3. ProPublica's Code of Ethics. www.propublica.org/about/code-of-ethics.

4. Interview with Leon Dash, January 27, 2009.

5. Todd Purdum, obituary for Robin Toner, *The New York Times,* December 13, 2008. Available online, http://topics.nytimes.com/ top/reference/timestopics/people/t/robin_toner/index.html. Accessed March 24, 2011.

# 5

Those who wish to succeed must ask the right preliminary questions.

ARISTOTLE, METAPHYSICS

# ask good questions

**K**atie Couric's approach was straightforward.

"Would you support a moratorium on foreclosures to help average Americans keep their homes?" the former *CBS Evening News* anchor asked Alaska's Governor Sarah Palin, who was the 2008 Republican candidate for vice president.

"That's something that John McCain and I have both been discussing, whether that . . . is part of the solution or not," answered Palin. "You know, it's going to be a multi-faceted solution that has to be found here."

Couric followed up. "What are the pros and cons of it, do you think?"

"Oh, well, some decisions that have been made poorly should not be rewarded, of course," Palin said.

"By consumers, you're saying?"

"Consumers—and those who were predator lenders also," Palin answered. "That's, you know that has to be considered also. But again, it's got to be a comprehensive, long-term solution found. . . . We are getting into crisis mode here."

In interviews over several days, Couric asked Palin about her foreign policy experience. Palin cited Alaska's proximity to Russia and a worry about flyovers by Russian Prime Minister Vladimir Putin. Couric asked the governor to name any

U. S. Supreme Court decisions other than *Roe v. Wade* that she disagreed with. Palin couldn't cite any. Couric asked Palin, a journalism major in college, to list the newspapers and magazines she read to stay informed about the world. Palin couldn't name one. Couric pressed Palin for examples of how her presidential running mate, Arizona Senator John McCain, had pushed for increased federal regulation of Wall Street. Palin kept hedging. Couric asked one last time.

"I'll try to find you some and I'll bring them to you," Palin answered.

In a final interview with McCain and Palin, Couric asked about a comment by Palin that contradicted McCain's position that the U. S. should not launch cross-border attacks from Afghanistan into Pakistan. McCain jumped to his runningmate's defense, saying Palin's words had been taken out of context.

"What did you learn from that experience?" Couric asked Palin.

"That this is all about 'gotcha' journalism," Palin answered.[1]

alin's interviews became a cause-célèbre during the 2008 presidential campaign. Many of her supporters agreed that she was a victim of "gotcha" journalism and that the questions posed to her were unfair and mean-spirited. In an interview on a conservative blog, Palin described many of the questions as cheap shots and said she was surprised at how journalism ethics had changed since her college days.[2]

The criticism prompted Kelly McBride of the Poynter Institute to ask a question of her own: What exactly was unfair about any of the questions that Couric asked?

"Hard questions are not gotcha journalism," McBride wrote in her online ethics column. "Pressing the potential vice president for details that might reveal the depth of her knowledge on the economy or foreign policy is not unethical. If anything, it is the exact opposite of unethical. . . . This is a job interview."[3]

### SUBSTANCE RATHER THAN STYLE

ohn Sawatsky, an award-winning journalist in Canada, investigated how journalists conduct interviews, and why some interviews succeed but many others fail. He studied the transcripts and recordings of thousands of interviews in an effort to change the culture of how journalists ask questions and conduct interviews.[4]

The successful interview, Sawatsky determined, depends more on the question-asker than on the answer-giver. A journalist's question should be a precise instrument, he says, but too often it is wielded haphazardly and thoughtlessly. Unprepared journalists improvise their interviews and find themselves at the mercy of their subjects. If the subject is friendly and takes pity on the journalist, the interview may yield something that is worthwhile and usable. If the subject is unfriendly or downright hostile, the result may be disastrous. The journalist will be left with little or nothing of substance.

According to Sawatsky, you as a journalist should:

- Ask open-ended, neutral questions that require your subject to provide details, explain unseen causes and clarify underlying motivations.

- Avoid charged language or loaded words. Your questions should not sound tough, but they should probe tough issues.

- Keep your questions short and focused. Don't overload them with details that will allow the subject to answer selectively.

Do not be fooled by many of the tough interviews that take place on network and cable television. Often, Sawatsky says, the interviewer is more interested in how he comes across to his audience than in the information he obtains. The focus is not on the subject of the interview but the interviewer, and the emphasis is on style rather than substance. The goal of such interviews is not journalism but entertainment.

Sawatsky says interviewers in those settings ask tough-sounding questions when they should be exploring tough issues. "Are you cheating on your wife?" may sound tough, but the answer will probably be "no." Instead, Sawatsky says you should ask the subject to describe his relationship with his wife, and then you should build on the answers:

*When was your last vacation together? Where did you go? What did you and your wife do together last weekend? How do you spend your free time? How do you feel about your wife?*

Sawatsky's technique requires the flexibility to build on the subject's answers. The effective journalist doesn't just recite a list of questions but engages with the interviewee. Asking good questions is the foundation of a successful interview.

## THE SUCCESSFUL INTERVIEW

ou will ask lots of questions as a journalist. You will ask people what they know, what they heard and saw, what they think and believe, and what they hope for. Doing it well requires practice and preparation. Good questions illuminate issues and capture the personality and character of the people you're writing about.

You may never interview a candidate for president or vice president on national television. But you will talk to candidates for local or state offices or people already elected to those posts. You'll spend time talking to cops on the beat and teachers and students in local schools. Most of the men and women you interview will not be famous or well connected but they will have become part of a news story, sometimes through circumstances beyond their control. You will ask your questions in widely varying sets of circumstances. You may find yourself doing a quick telephone interview to nail down information about an accident, a crime or a governmental action. You may be at the scene of a breaking news story competing with other reporters for information. Or you may be working on a major profile or investigative piece and have the opportunity to conduct a lengthy sit-down interview with the subject of your story.

Some interviewees will be friendly. Some will be contentious. You'll be prepared for some interviews, but others will come on short notice, with little opportunity to consider all the questions you should ask. Imagine any scenario and you'll probably experience it sooner or later.

### Talking to strangers

The first hurdle may come well before you ask your first question. Interviewing people requires you to approach people you don't know, something that may be outside your comfort zone. You may discover that talking to people you have never met before is the most challenging part of your job as a beginning journalist. Success requires that you conquer your fear of approaching and talking to strangers.

Novelist and journalist Tom Wolfe described the difficulty this way: "The initial problem," Wolfe said, "is always to approach a total stranger, move in on their lives in some fashion, ask questions you have no natural right to expect answers to, ask to see things you weren't meant to see, and so on. Many journalists find it so ungentlemanly, so embarrassing, so terrifying even, that they are never able to master the first step."

Inexperienced journalists may lack confidence to approach someone they don't know, especially about matters that are sensitive or even private. You may be convinced that someone will not talk to you, and then be surprised to find out how eager people are to share their stories, even in stressful situations or when talking to the media may not be in the person's best interests. The key is, you won't know whether someone will talk until you ask. Be bold. You'll be turned down sometimes, but you'll find that many people are willing to tell what they saw, what they heard, and what happened to them.

Don't avoid a direct conversation by resorting to an e-mail interview. E-mails don't allow you to adjust your questions as needed or to explore important details. The format is prone to misinterpretation, both by you and the person you are interviewing. Use e-mail to verify facts and details, but not to discuss personal or emotional issues.

## Preparing for the interview

Preparation breeds confidence, so plan your interview as thoroughly as you can. Think carefully about the topics you want to cover and write out your questions beforehand if you have time. Ask them critically as you talk to the person you're interviewing, trying to anticipate follow-up questions you may need to ask that you hadn't initially considered.

You may not have a lot of time to get ready, of course. Starting out as a journalist, most of your interviews will probably come on short notice, and you will need to prepare yourself as quickly and as thoroughly as you can. A quick search of old stories in your organization's electronic morgue or paper archives will turn up background information to help you understand a person or an issue. Don't hesitate to use Google, Bing or another Internet search engine to find a resume or other stories about your subject. Even a little bit of background information can prove useful and give you ideas about things to look for and questions to ask. Of course, use any information that you find online carefully. Verify anything that you haven't gathered independently.

## Approaching your subject

Part of a successful interview is explaining who you are and what your job is, especially if you're interviewing someone unaccustomed to talking to a reporter. Help the person understand why you're interested in her story, and assure her that you'll do your best to tell her story fairly and accurately, even if you have to ask hard questions about topics she might not like. Help her understand how readers or viewers might react to her story. And always get a phone number rather than an e-mail address so you can call back if you need to double-check a fact or ask a follow-up question. Phone calls are faster and more reliable; e-mails can be missed or ignored.

Be honest and straightforward and treat your subject with respect and dignity. An interview is a partnership. Your subject has a story and you want to tell it. She'll know if you're trying to manipulate her, so being forthright increases the likelihood that she'll tell you things you really need to know.

Your most uncomfortable interview may entail talking to someone who's experienced a personally devastating or traumatic experience, perhaps the death of a family member or friend. You will need to balance your journalistic mission with respect and compassion for this individual. Never forget that you're talking to a real person with feelings and emotions. Treat him fairly and honestly.

- Make sure the person understands you're a journalist, and identify the organization you work for.

- If you're talking about someone who has died or been killed, explain that you want your readers or viewers to know what the person was like, what kind of life she lived, and what was important to her.

- Respect your subject's emotions; crying is not a sign of weakness but a normal response to trauma.

- Give your subject the time he needs to gain his composure and answer your questions.

- Prepare yourself for your own emotional response to a traumatic story. You will inevitably come away from such stories with a mixture of emotions, which is natural. You're human, and you've got feelings, too. Don't ignore them.

- Don't ask the grieving person, *how does it feel?* It's an easy but foolish question that people are hard-pressed to answer with any real meaning.

### Honing the conversational interview

Your most comfortable interviews may seem less like work and more like a conversation. Your subject has a story to tell, and you simply let her talk. A master of this form of interview was Studs Terkel, the Pulitzer-Prize winning author who chronicled the stories of Americans in a dozen books, collecting accounts about the Great Depression, World War II and the everyday lives of working men and women. He loved conversations in which his subjects discovered things about themselves that they had not realized before. In a *NewsHour* segment on PBS, Terkel recalled a tape-recorded interview with an unmarried mother of four who lived in a Chicago housing project:

"We play it back and she hears her voice and she says something, suddenly puts her hand to her mouth and says, 'Oh, my God!' I said, 'What is it?' She said, 'I never knew I felt that way before.'

"Well, bingo, that's a star for her and for me." In other words, that interview helped her say something that revealed herself to herself.

"It's not an interview; it's a conversation," Terkel continued. "You, yourself, enter it, too. I'm not the guy from *60 Minutes* coming down to talk to them."[5]

The best question, Terkel often said, was a simple one: *And then? What happened next?*

Andre Schiffrin, his longtime editor, said that people would tell Terkel the truth even when they had lied to themselves for their whole lives. "The key thing was his respect for them," Schiffrin recalled in a news story after Terkel died in 2008. "He wasn't there to use them. He wasn't there to make a point. He really wanted to hear what they had to say, and he respected them."[6]

For Terkel, these sessions weren't interviews. He was just talking to people, though for a special purpose. He said the journalist's job is to try to see the world through the eyes of the people he or she is talking to, if only for a day.

Terkel's conversational interview skills were, of course, honed over decades of talking and listening to people about the things important to them. As a new journalist, you may consider his techniques easy and quickly learned. Don't be fooled: they require as much careful preparation and discipline as any interview. Don't try to wing it through even the friendliest, most non-threatening encounter. The more prepared you are, the easier it will seem. Your job is to listen— and to listen well, a skill that will be discussed further in Chapter 6. Be genuinely interested and curious about what your subject thinks and does, but remember that when you're talking he isn't. Keep your mouth shut most of the time.

When you do speak, frame your questions carefully by making sure they're designed to draw out information, not shut it off. Paraphrase what you've heard and ask if you've understood everything correctly. Finally, trust your intuition; if something doesn't sound or feel right, ask additional questions in an effort to clarify and understand what's really going on.

## Handling the difficult interview

Not all interviews can be Terkel-like conversations, of course. Sometimes you will be faced with a difficult interview, someone who is at the top of her game and dead-set on keeping you from finding out what you want to know. You may be talking to a public relations person or a spin doctor intent on getting across her argument or point of view; she may ignore your questions and provide answers to questions she would have preferred you to ask. Your subject may be a public official who is trying to keep something hidden. Or you may be talking to someone who simply doesn't trust journalists and wants nothing to do with you.

The best questions for these occasions are informed ones, says two-time Pulitzer Prize winner Eric Nalder of *The Seattle Times*. You need to bone up on the specifics of the topic in question and read or view what your subject has said about it previously. Approach your subject only after careful planning, which may require rehearsing the questions you want to ask.

Have confidence that you'll get the information you're after, Nalder says. Reporters who don't believe they will get the interview almost always fail.

"As far as I'm concerned, no one should ever refuse to talk to me," Nalder writes in "Loosening Lips," his guide to the art of the interview. "It works."[7]

## CONCLUSION

Eric Nalder, John Sawatsky and other skilled interviewers preach preparation and methodology. As with everything you do in journalism, the more prepared you are for your interviews—even the friendly ones—the better your results will be.

But preparation does not mean blindly following your list of planned questions. It also means anticipating the course of the interview and being ready to make a quick change depending on what your subject says. According to Sawatsky a good interview is built on the answers that the subject gives, not just on the prepared questions. You must be flexible, alert and attentive to what is said and, often, to what is left out. If your subject makes assertions, probe for more details and evidence. Use your questions as a roadmap for the interview, but do not let them prevent you from taking interesting and important side trips.

Take into account how much time you have for your interview with a difficult subject. You may find yourself with barely a half-hour; often it will be much less. In those situations, your questions need to be well ordered and tightly focused. Ask questions that deal with matters that are not already known or are not already on the record.

If your interview subject is particularly savvy, he may go off on a rhetorical tangent and ignore your well-formed question to talk about his own issues, not yours. When that happens, be polite but ask your question again firmly. Never hesitate to ask for more elaboration or explanation.

Always remember your goals as a journalist, in the interviews you conduct and the stories you write and produce. "Journalism," Sawatsky told *American Journalism Review,* "is about directness, precision, clarity, about not confusing people. . . . Questions are supposed to get answers. Questions that fail to get answers are not tough enough."

Your job in an interview is to gather new information and details about the person or the subject you're writing about. You've succeeded when you produce something new and enlightening.

## checklist

- **Be yourself.** Learn from the master interviewers, but don't try to be Katie Couric or John Sawatsky. Find your voice as an interviewer and be comfortable with it.

- **Choose the right setting.** Offices are sometimes the most appropriate and convenient place for an interview, but they can be filled with distractions and interruptions. Outdoors can be noisy. Homes are great because many people are comfortable talking at their own kitchen table.

- **Tap into your subject's ability to remember.** Ask him to try to recall specific details and events. Ask him about what the weather was like, what he was wearing, what he remembers seeing and hearing.

- **Don't be afraid to admit that you don't understand something.** If something isn't clear, clarify it. The only stupid question is the one you don't ask. Your source will appreciate your efforts to accurately understand and report what he tells you.

- **Always ask *why.*** *"Why* did you do this?" *"Why* were you there?"

- **Take notes.** Even if you're recording the interview, take brief notes. They'll help you organize your thoughts so you don't have to review the complete recording. (Your notes will come in handy, too, if your recorder malfunctions.)

- **Don't be late.** You get only one chance to make a good first impression. Don't blow it with someone you've never met before.

Arrive early and use the extra time to collect your thoughts and think through your interview.

- **Dress appropriately.** You want to be taken seriously? Dress neatly. If you dress like a sloppy college student, that's how you'll be treated. But don't overdress, either. You may need to describe your subject's clothes, but you don't want her talking about how you were dressed after you've gone.

- **Be professional.** Don't yawn, don't look at your watch and be sure to turn off your phone.

- **Make your last question count.** Pulitzer Prize-winner David Halberstam said the best question any reporter can ask is: "Who else should I see?" Film critic Gene Siskel would end interviews by asking, "What do you know for sure?"

## assignments

Watch an interview conducted by a single network or cable newsperson. Then analyze the questions based on John Sawatsky's techniques:

1. How many of the questions are open-ended, and how many could be answered with a *yes* or *no?*

2. How focused are the questions?

3. Does the interviewer give too much detail in his questions, leading the interviewee in a particular direction?

4. How good are the follow-up questions?

5. Do the follow-up questions build on answers, or do they appear to follow an inflexible outline?

6. What new information did you take away from the interview?

## notes

1. Katie Couric, interviews with Sarah Palin and Joe Biden, *CBS Evening News,* September–October, 2008. Available online, www.cbsnews.com/stories/2008/09/24/eveningnews/ main4476173.shtml; www.cbsnews.com/stories/2008/10/01/ eveningnews/main4493062.shtml; www.cbsnews.com/stories/ 2008/09/25/eveningnews/main4479062.shtml; www.cbsnews.

com/stories/2008/09/30/eveningnews/main4490618.shtml;
www.cbsnews.com/stories/2008/09/29/eveningnews/main
4487826.shtml. Accessed March 29, 2011.

2. Sarah Palin made her comments to Hugh Hewitt for his September
   30, 2008, Townhall.com blog. http://townhall.com/columnists/
   hughhewitt/2008/09/30/sarah_palin_i_know_what_americans_
   are_going_through.

3. Kelly McBride, "Everyday Ethics," at Poynter.org. October 1,
   2008. Available online at www.poynter.org/column.asp?id=67&
   aid=151526. Accessed March 29, 2011.

4. Susan Paterno, "The Question Man." *American Journalism Review* (October 2000); David Folkenflik, profile of John Sawatsky,
   *All Things Considered,* August 14, 2006. Available online. www.
   npr.org/templates/story/story.php?storyId=5625218. Accessed
   March 29, 2011.

5. Terence Smith, interview with Studs Terkel and Alex Kotlowitz.
   *NewsHour,* August 3, 2005. Available online. www.pbs.org/
   newshour/bb/entertainment/july-dec05/studs_8-03.html. Accessed March 29, 2011.

6. Andre Schiffrin was quoted in Stephanie Simon's October 31,
   2008, story about Studs Terkel's death in the *Los Angeles Times.*
   www.latimes.com/news/obituaries/la-me-terkel1-2008nov01,0,
   3697875,full.story.

7. Eric Nalder, "Loosening Lips," Committee of Concerned
   Journalists, July 9, 2007. Available online. www.concerned
   journalists.org/loosening-lips. Accessed March 29, 2011.

# 6

When we were young, we were told that poetry is about voice, about finding a voice and speaking with this voice, but the older I get I think it's not about voice, it's about listening and the art of listening, listening with attention. I don't just mean with the ear; bringing the quality of attention to the world. The writers I like best are those who attend.

KATHLEEN JAMIE, SCOTTISH POET[1]

# listen with attention

Early each semester Leon Dash gave his journalism students at the University of Illinois a taste of the interviewing techniques he had honed over more than thirty years as a *Washington Post* reporter. He paired students together and instructed each to question the other about their earliest school memories.

One student told her partner about growing up in southern India. Even though she was Hindu she had been sent to a Catholic school for first grade, and she described how students were required to wear a different uniform to class each day.

The Indian student finished her story, and her interviewer began to ask about her experiences in second grade.

*No, no, no,* Dash said, interrupting the questioner. Ask how she got back and forth to school. Her parents weren't going to let a five- or six-year-old girl walk to school by herself.

The student said an auto rickshaw took her to school each day.

Satisfied with the answer, her interviewer again prepared to move on.

*No, no, no,* Dash repeated. Ask who drove the rickshaw; was it someone in her family?

The interviewer followed Dash's directions. The Indian student said her family hired a driver to take her to and from school every day.

For Dash this was a teachable moment. In just a few minutes, he asked his students, what has she told us about herself? Even if you don't know the intricacies of Indian society, what have you been able to learn?

No one seemed to know.

Dash provided the answers. She comes from an elite family, he said. How many Catholic schools require a different uniform every day? How many kids who go to a Catholic school can afford a different uniform every day?

She's Hindu, Dash continued, but she's going to a Catholic school because her parents obviously believe that's where she'll get a quality education. They have the money to pay for a driver to pick her up, take her to school and bring her home again every day.

That's not the average Indian family, Dash continued, it's an elite family. You've picked all of that up in just a few minutes.

With, of course, considerable prodding from Dash.[2]

ash's method of interviewing is designed to help students in his immersion journalism class examine contemporary social phenomena through the lives of individuals and families. By semester's end his students will have spent twenty or more hours interviewing subjects about their first school memories, their earliest recollections of family life, their religious upbringings and, finally, their lives on their own. Dash says the methodology can be used to examine living conditions, family histories and attitudes of any ethnic group at any class level.

Dash devised his methodology to satisfy his own curiosity about why people turn out the way they do and where and how they fit into society. People give us a universe in their answers to our questions, Dash says, and he tries to teach students how to see and hear those universes in the answers to the questions they ask. He believes curious students can extract surprising revelations about their subjects' needs, desires and motivations. Most importantly, students can learn how the personalities, the circumstances, and the choices made by parents and forebears still have bearing on the lives of the profile subjects today.

Dash teaches his students how to ask questions for long-form journalism. But he also teaches them to be alert to the context of what is revealed by the answers they're given, and to be attentive to the nuances of what is left unsaid.

Dash teaches his students how to listen. It may be one of the most important lessons they learn.

## YOU'RE NOT THE FOCUS OF THE INTERVIEW

**Y**ou can distinguish yourself as a journalist by asking good questions, but you will excel only when you listen carefully to people's answers.

Listening well is not something that comes naturally to most of us. It's a skill that must be developed, and few of us take the time to master it. Pay attention to almost any conversation going on around you and you'll see that few people are truly interested in listening to what someone else says. More often, each person is thinking about what he will say next, if he's paying attention to the conversation at all.

Good listening is important in all aspects of our lives. If you don't listen carefully to your professor in class—or worse, if you doze off—you may miss an assignment and fail the final exam. You could lose your job if you don't pay attention to your boss. Personal relationships also hinge on effective communication; if you don't listen to what your partner or spouse tells you and vice versa, your relationship will suffer.

Listening well is also essential to your success as a journalist. Robert Stevenson, an associate professor of journalism at Lander University in Greenwood, South Carolina, tells students that listening well is the first step toward improving their reporting and writing. He describes the subtle but important difference between hearing and listening. Hearing, he says, is to listening as talking is to public speaking; hearing and talking come naturally, but listening and public speaking take training and practice. Reporters, he says, must be active listeners, listening not for entertainment but for comprehension. Reporters who do this well consider *what* is being said as well as *how* and *why* it's being said. The good reporter also listens analytically, Stevenson says, thinking critically about whether the information is valid or not.[3]

You can miss the real story if you don't listen well. During an interview you may be in such a hurry to get to the next question that you fail to pick up on an important detail your subject has revealed. You may simply ask questions by rote and miss a subtle comment that, if explored, could provide enlightenment. For example, without prodding from Dash, his students would have missed the most important details about their Indian classmate by hurrying through their questions and not analyzing her answers.

Avoid making these related mistakes:

- Finding your subject boring.
- Thinking you already know the answers to the questions you're going to ask.

- Believing nothing your subject says will change your opinion of the topic at hand.

- Focusing too hard on taking notes to the point that you fail to notice the subtext of what is being said.

Sometimes you may simply lose sight of your goal and end up talking more than the person you're interviewing. This means you're showing off and you have become the focus of the interview instead of the person you're talking to.

"Using a tape recorder taught me my most important lesson of interviewing: to shut up," says the Poynter Institute's Chip Scanlan. "It was a painful learning experience, having to listen to myself stepping on people's words, cutting them off just as they were getting enthusiastic or appeared about to make a revealing statement. There were far too many times I heard myself asking overly long and leading questions, instead of simply saying, 'Why?' or 'How did it happen?' or 'When did all this begin?' or 'What do you mean?' and then closing my mouth and letting people answer."[4]

Your purpose as a journalist is to find out what someone else knows. You don't learn anything when you do most of the talking.

Journalists aren't the only professionals who often don't listen well. In an essay for National Public Radio, Dr. Alicia Conill, a clinical associate professor at the University of Pennsylvania School of Medicine, said studies have shown it takes about 18 seconds for a physician to interrupt a patient who is talking, and she gave an example from her own experience. Conill was on her hospital rounds one day and made her last stop at the bedside of an elderly woman. The woman asked Conill to help her put on her socks. Instead of listening, the doctor looked at the woman's charts, and then launched into her own monologue.

In a stern voice, the woman stopped Conill. "Sit down, doctor. This is my story, not your story."[5]

## SHARPENING YOUR LISTENING SKILLS

 ow can you become a good listener? First, remember you're not the focus of the interview. Concentrate on the person you're talking to and give your full attention to everything she says. You can facilitate this by:

- **Not writing everything down.** That's what your recorder is for. Instead, jot down key words or phrases and use them to formulate your next questions.

- **Not interrupting.** Let a silence linger. Many people are uncomfortable with silence and will continue talking unprompted, offering unsolicited and often surprising information.

- **Paying attention to your subject's body language.** When your subject in a face-to-face interview seems nervous or distracted, try to ease her worries or concerns.

- **Paying attention to your own body language.** You're not there just to take transcription. Let your subject know you're engaged in what he's saying. Make eye contact and respond when appropriate.

- **Not hurrying your subject.** Let him answer your questions and let him finish his own sentences. To do otherwise suggests that you already know what your subject is going to say when, in fact, you don't. Also, don't hint at what you believe about the topic.

Finally, remember there is more to an answer than spoken words. Emotions and feelings may be communicated by nonverbal means. Being a good listener means paying attention with all of your senses, not just your sense of hearing.

## LISTENING PAYS OFF

You won't know what your story is about until you've really listened and paid attention to what's going on around you. Eudora Welty was a journalist before she wrote her great short stories and novels. As a child growing up in Mississippi, she listened for stories long before she ever thought about becoming a writer. Listening *for* stories, she said, is something much more acute than listening *to* them.[6]

Walt Harrington also listens for stories. Harrington, a colleague of Dash's at both *The Washington Post* and the University of Illinois, is a proponent of what he calls *intimate journalism,* which he describes as stories about the everyday lives of ordinary people, told in a distinctive voice and with many extraordinary details. Harrington's secret to reaching depth and breadth in his stories lies in convincing his subjects that the story is a partnership that will succeed only if the subject is enthusiastically involved. Harrington begins his interviews as conversations in which he lets people ramble on about their lives to see where they go. "Cast a wide net," he writes in his book *Intimate Journalism.* "See what rises forth."[7]

Harrington believes people "are willing to show their vulnerabilities to those who reveal their own vulnerabilities," and says it's okay to talk about yourself, your friends, your wife or husband, your kids. In intimate interviews, Harrington writes, you don't ask a question only once. You ask it in different ways and at different times, and you listen carefully to the answer each time.

Dana Priest and Anne Hull say listening well was an essential element in their *Washington Post* series about conditions that injured soldiers and Marines were forced to endure at Walter Reed Army Medical Center. Hull said much of the early reporting for their stories, which won the 2008 Pulitzer Prize for public service, began with the reporters simply hanging out with people who had been treated at Walter Reed.[8] The more Hull and Priest observed, the more they began to understand the neglect suffered by the injured soldiers and the impact this neglect had on their lives and the lives of their families. Hull told the 2008 Nieman Conference on Narrative Journalism how she and Priest went to a hotel bar on the military post where injured soldiers would gather to drink, sometimes all night.

"We sat there and watched for a couple of hours and took it in," Hull said. "We just wanted to get a sense of this place. We would continually go back to the bar and listen to who might have been complaining or who seemed extra frustrated. And when that soldier went away from the crowd, maybe went back to his room or went outside to smoke, we'd find a way to talk to that soldier and say, 'We've heard there are some things going on here. We're newspaper reporters. Would you care to talk to us about it?' That's how we'd test the water to see if that soldier wanted to talk."

Priest continued: "One of the things that I learned in doing this story is the importance of listening. It sounds like such a basic thing, but we're in this era of journalism in which a lot of journalists are doing the talking and often talking about derivative information. But the art of listening is so fundamental to what we do. And if you have a heightened ability to do that, and a heightened sense of that importance, you can pick up so much. That person standing there, reading his body language, not a complainer, macho guy, not supposed to be wounded, not feeling comfortable enough to tell us the whole truth about [Walter Reed] because he didn't even know us. But there is just so much in his voice, and in the voices of a lot of people that we would talk with even though we didn't know their whole stories. So I tell myself when I start new projects, just listen, and it does pay off."

## CONCLUSION

Listening to people—really listening to them—proves you are interested in what they have to say. You're flattered when someone is truly interested in what you think. Show your subjects the same interest and courtesy, and they're more likely to continue telling you interesting things about themselves and issues that are important to both of you.

Reporters who listen well exhibit humility, a characteristic not often associated with journalists. Ken Auletta, who writes about the media for *The New Yorker,* says humility is important because "it aids two of a journalist's irreplaceable tools: the curiosity to ask questions and the ability to listen to the answers. Each requires modesty because each requires us not to assume that we already know the answers."[9]

The first step in learning, Socrates said, is to know what you do not know. As a beginning journalist, remember this. No matter how much you've researched and prepared, no matter how much you think you know about the issue you're planning to write about, you still do not know it all. You may, in fact, know very little. Listen to the answers your interviewees provide, and you'll be constantly surprised by what you learn.

### checklist

- **Focus on your subject.** She's the reason for the interview, not you.
- **Remember that listening is more than simply hearing.** Use all of your senses. Pay attention to your subject's body language, and yours, too.
- **Don't be afraid of silence.** Use it to your advantage by waiting for your subject to break it.
- **Be respectful.** Turn off the cell phone and don't check for text messages or look at your watch as if you're bored. Give your subject the attention she deserves.
- **Stay humble.** You may be prepared, but you don't know the answers to your questions yet.

### assignments

1. Videotape one of your interviews. Play it back and take notes on your techniques. What kinds of questions did you ask? Were you

asking open-ended or closed questions? Did you offer cues to your subject about possible answers to your questions? Did you frame your follow-up questions based on the answers you were given, or did you blindly follow a script? How relaxed did you seem? How attentive were you to your subject's body language?

2. Calculate how much time you spent talking and how much time you gave your subject to answer your questions. Did you spend more time talking than your subject? How do you think the balance of time between your questions and the subject's answers affected how much you got out of the interview?

## notes

1. Kirsty Scott, "Kathleen Jamie: In Conversation with the Natural World." *The Guardian* (UK), June 18, 2005. Available online. www.guardian.co.uk/books/2005/jun/18/featuresreviews. guardianreview15.

2. Leon Dash was interviewed on January 27, 2009.

3. Robert Stevenson, "Effective Listening: The First Step to Improving Writing." *The Collegiate Journalist*, 36(1) (fall 2006). Available online. www.scj.us/tcj/articles/fall06_stevenson2.shtml. Accessed April 4, 2011.

4. Chip Scanlan, "Chip on Your Shoulder" blog, Poynter.org, July 3, 2003. www.poynter.org/how-tos/newsgathering-storytelling/chip-on-your-shoulder/13140/the-power-of-listening/.

5. Alicia Conill, "Listening Is Powerful Medicine," *Weekend Edition Sunday,* National Public Radio, February 1, 2009. Available online. www.npr.org/templates/story/story.php?storyId=100062673. Accessed April 4, 2011.

6. Eudora Welty, *One Writer's Beginnings.* Harvard University Press, 1984, p. 14.

7. Walt Harrington, "A Writer's Essay: Seeking the Extraordinary in the Ordinary," in *Intimate Journalism: The Art and Craft of Reporting Everyday Life.* Sage Publications, 1997, pp. xvii–xlvi.

8. Dana Priest and Anne Hull, *Nieman Reports,* summer 2008. Available online. www.nieman.harvard.edu/reportsitem. aspx?id=100033. Accessed April 4, 2011.

9. Ken Auletta, *Backstory: Inside the Business of News,* Penguin, 2003, introduction; "Whom Do Journalists Work For?" Red Smith Lecture in Journalism, Notre Dame University, 2005.

I tell musicians, "Don't trust nobody but your mama. And even then, look at her real good."

BO DIDDLEY,
ROCK AND BLUES LEGEND

# be skeptical

Reporters from around the country camped out for two days in Sago, West Virginia, covering the story of 13 coal miners trapped by an explosion two miles inside a mine. News developments came at an agonizingly slow pace. Rescue crews had to wait 12 hours before they could enter the mine because of high levels of carbon monoxide and methane gas. Once inside they moved carefully, checking for seeping water, unstable roof conditions and dangerous gas buildups. The miners' families gathered at a local church to wait and pray. Outside, newspaper, radio and television reporters kept their own vigil, providing around-the-clock coverage of the disaster.

As midnight approached, surprising news began to spread throughout the community. Almost 40 hours after the explosion, rescuers had reached the trapped miners. Word was that one miner was dead, but 12 had miraculously survived. West Virginia Governor Joe Manchin was in Sago and said he'd also heard the good news. With a hint of caution, CNN first reported that family members had been alerted to the rescue. Within 15 minutes the network presented the survival of the 12 miners as fact. "There is elation at this moment," Anderson Cooper said.

Other television networks and National Public Radio carried similar bulletins. Up against deadlines for their morning editions, newspapers made the rescue their lead story. "Miracle in Mine," read the headline in the *Atlanta Journal-Constitution,* while *USA Today* proclaimed " 'Alive' Miners Beat Odds." Family members and Sago residents began to celebrate.

But something didn't seem right to Becky Wagoner, a reporter for *The Inter-Mountain,* a small daily newspaper in nearby Elkins. She was the first reporter to reach the mine after the explosion. A native of the coalfields, she knew some of the miners and their families and many of the people involved in the rescue. She had stationed herself at the media information center, where company officials had provided regular but gloomy news updates. Now the news was apparently good, but the officials were saying nothing; they weren't even at the media center. Wagoner was skeptical. Where were they and why weren't they talking? She also heard that 12 ambulances had arrived at the mine entrance, but only one had driven away. Why was that?

Stories began to circulate. One report said the ambulances were taking the survivors to the church to meet their families. Wagoner knew that didn't make sense from a medical standpoint, but emotions were high and everyone latched onto the optimistic reports.

The truth slowly emerged. Instead of 12 survivors, only one miner was alive— a miracle, yes, but not the one trumpeted via radio, television and newspapers around the country.[1]

The Associated Press moved a bulletin with the corrected story, but it was too late for many papers in the East and Midwest. *The Rocky Mountain News* in Denver stopped its press run and discarded 10,000 copies with the erroneous story. CNN was the first cable channel to correct the story, nearly three hours after its initial report.

Ralph Hanson, then a journalism professor at West Virginia University, went to bed the night before listening to reports that the miners were alive. When he read the AP account of the rescue in the morning paper, he knew something wasn't right. It cited only one official—the governor—who never identified the source of his information by name. The report provided no details on the miners or where they were found, and the story concluded with the detail that the mining company had not confirmed the rescues.[2]

Warning bells failed to go off for many of the reporters at Sago.

Hanson studied how the news coverage went so wrong. News organizations faced tight deadlines, but they should have been clearer about the unconfirmed nature of their reports. News organizations, he says, have become too complacent about passing along stories that are merely rumors. No longer do the stories have to be true; it just has to be true that the story is out there.

A miraculous rescue of the miners was what the country wanted to hear. When the initial erroneous reports came out, many reporters and their editors were swept up in the euphoria of the moment, and they failed to abide by one of journalism's cardinal rules: They did not check the story out.

"Most everybody took everything that was coming out as gospel," Wagoner said of the confusion that night. "A lot of people didn't take time to stop and think about what we were hearing."

Wagoner had stayed on the phone with her editor. They kept waiting for some official word, but it never came. They had an advantage because their paper had an afternoon deadline, but they resisted the temptation to post an online story about the rescue. In the end, the *Inter-Mountain* got the story right, both in print and on its website.

You can never be too skeptical of the stories you're told as a journalist, of the documents you've been given and even of things that you've seen or heard firsthand. Refusing to make assumptions or jump to conclusions will protect you as you sort truth from lies, facts from rumors and relevant details from insignificant fluff. Skepticism will keep you from jumping on bandwagons and making careless and embarrassing mistakes that undermine your credibility and that of the organization you work for. Your job is to clarify and explain, but you cannot do that if you haven't confirmed your stories by checking and double-checking all your sources of your information.

## CHECK HUMAN SOURCES

Be on guard against those who willfully lie, hide or shade the truth. Also be alert to people who are convinced they know what happened but don't. They will tell you what they believe or what they've heard from someone else. These accounts may be speculative or even wishful. Ask this key question: "How do you know?" It will allow you to test their accounts for accuracy and completeness through subsequent questions, research and reporting.

You are responsible not to your sources but to the readers and viewers who trust what you tell them. Maintain good relationships with your sources, of course, but don't write or produce stories with the sole aim of pleasing them. If someone gives you information, it's not rude to ask for details that will verify the authenticity of that information. Ask:

- How do you know this?
- Where can I find out more about this?
- Who can tell me something else about this subject?

■ Where can I find pertinent documents and records?

■ Where can I go to see for myself the things you've described?

Make it clear to your source that your sole objective is to tell the story as completely and accurately as possible, and that means you must ask additional questions and take nothing at face value.

For profiles of individuals, always research the person independently of your interview. Spot-check his credentials by calling places he said he worked or went to school. The higher the honor or the achievement, the more you need to verify its authenticity. For example, the Congressional Medal of Honor Society (CMOHS) maintains an archive of all recipients, including a separate list of living medal winners, on its website. It's quick and easy to check, but how many people would think to question a self-proclaimed Congressional Medal of Honor winner? As a journalist, you need to be one of those people.

Don't assume others have followed up on a story's details. If someone gives you an alibi, make sure the information checks out. One of the last living suspects in the 1963 church bombing that killed four schoolgirls in Birmingham, Alabama, claimed he'd been home watching wrestling on TV when the attack took place. Reporter Jerry Mitchell of the Jackson, Mississippi, *Clarion-Ledger* has won numerous awards for his investigations of crimes committed during the civil-rights era. Skeptical of this alibi, he checked the TV listings in old newspapers; no wrestling was broadcast at that time. "For three and a half decades, his alibi had gone unchallenged," Mitchell said.[3]

Eyewitnesses are great sources, but approach their information with skepticism. Two people who experience the same event may provide startlingly different accounts. Talk to the first responders on the scene of the wreck or fire, but also look for people who showed up later as well. They'll add information to round out the story and make it more complete. Use the tips discussed in Chapter 5 to formulate good questions that will draw out concrete details about an event, and avoid asking questions that will elicit broad generalizations—or worse, just a *yeah* or a *nope*. The more specific the details and the more similarities you find in separate accounts, the more confident you can be in your reporting.

Attribute information from your sources carefully and precisely. Independently verifying everything you've been told may not be possible under a tight deadline, so it's important to explain exactly where you got your information and what steps you took to try to confirm it.

## CHECK DOCUMENTS AND RECORDS

**A**pply the same tough standards of verification to the documents and records you use in your stories as you do to the people you quote. Citing an official record gives you confidence, and you can certainly enjoy the legal privilege attached to such documents. But records and documents can be as false as human sources precisely because humans prepare them. A police report may be based on an eyewitness who really didn't see everything she claimed to see. A data clerk may have transposed numbers on a spreadsheet. A court clerk may have transcribed data incorrectly, or a court reporter may have misspelled someone's name. A sworn statement may be based on a hazy recollection, a faulty perception or a willful intent to mislead. Be as skeptical of records and documents as you are of the people you interview. Check and double-check all of your information, no matter where it comes from.

Good reporters understand the importance of having what Brant Houston, who holds the Knight Chair in Investigative Reporting in the Department of Journalism at the University of Illinois, calls a "documents state of mind."[4] In *The Investigative Reporter's Handbook: A Guide to Documents, Databases and Techniques,* Houston provides guidelines for finding and verifying information in primary documents such as lawsuits, transcripts of legislative hearings or campaign finance reports. Houston drills his students on the importance of interviewing documents just as they would interview a human subject. He urges them to find people who can explain what the document really means and put it in context. This may be the person who created the document in the first place, or it may be the custodian of the document. It may be an outside expert who has a deep understanding of events or issues that led to the document's creation. While you can safely quote from an official document, always to try to find an independent and authoritative source to help explain it clearly and concisely to your readers or viewers.

## USING OBJECTIVE, SCIENTIFIC METHODS TO CHECK YOUR WORK

**S**peed does not always complement skepticism. You have deadlines to meet, and you want to stay ahead of your competition on important stories. But don't let deadlines force you into writing something you don't know for certain. A skeptical reporter must work fast, but more importantly she must work care-

The winner of the 1995 Miss Virginia Pageant had a wonderful story of persistence: She'd finally won the pageant in her fourth year of competition. Her resume was exceptional. In high school she'd been a star athlete and honor graduate, and now she was Phi Beta Kappa and a magna cum laude graduate of Virginia Tech. She'd been accepted to law school, and her ambition was to find ways to help poor children get to college.

Shannon Harrington, a reporting intern that summer at *The Roanoke Times,* covered the pageant and wrote about the winner, listing all her achievements. But the winner's story quickly began to unravel.

Phi Beta Kappa officials at Virginia Tech said she was not a member of the honorary society. Harrington began to check other parts of her resume and discovered they were not true, either. She tried to explain the discrepancies as simple misunderstandings, but the damage was done. The pageant board demanded her crown, and she eventually resigned.

Harrington was new to journalism. It didn't occur to him that a Miss Virginia contestant might embellish her resume, but his editors should have anticipated this possibility and required reporters to routinely check out biographical sketches. Major discrepancies, inconsistencies and misstatements would likely have surfaced if the most important parts of the resumes, such as claims of academic honors, public service, professional experience, post-graduate plans, had been merely spot-checked.

Harrington stuck with the story, and at the end of the summer his good work garnered him a full-time job with the paper. Years later when he was a financial reporter for Bloomberg News, he reflected on the lesson of the Miss Virginia story, which served as a wake-up call early in his career about the importance of being skeptical of everything he was told, no matter who told him or where it came from.[5]

fully. If you don't have all the answers you need for a story, make that fact clear to your readers. Good reporters are willing to admit what they don't know.

Use common sense, too. Sometimes you'll have to rely on your judgment to sort through conflicting information. Think logically about what you've seen and heard. The philosophical principle of Occam's razor says the simplest explanation is usually the correct one. But it may not be. Your job is to check it out and find out what's right.

Journalism is a discipline of verification, according to Bill Kovach and Tom Rosenstiel in *The Elements of Journalism.* Your task is to correctly report what has happened by adopting an objective methodology that, if not strictly scientific, comes close to that standard.[6]

Kovach and Rosenstiel take pains to clarify what they mean by *journalistic objectivity*. Too often, the term suggests that journalists should be free of bias, leaning neither one way nor the other. But we all are subject to biases, consciously or unconsciously. Your goal is to report stories in ways that take those biases out of play so they do not contaminate the information you present. Journalistic objectivity, Kovach and Rosenstiel say, requires you to develop "a consistent method of testing information—a transparent approach to evidence—precisely so that personal and cultural biases" do not undermine the accuracy of your work.

For Kovach and Rosenstiel, the intellectual principles of the science of reporting include:

- Never adding anything that was not there to begin with.
- Never deceiving your audience.
- Being as transparent as possible about your methods and motives.
- Relying on your own original reporting.
- Being humble, remaining skeptical of your own understanding, and continuing to question your conclusions.

Follow the evidence as a scientist would. Abandon your pet theory when the facts don't support it. Nobel Prize–winning physicist Richard Feynman said the scientific method is made up of three parts: observation, reason and experiment. A theory must satisfy all three elements, especially the experiment. "It doesn't matter how beautiful your theory is, it doesn't matter how smart you are. If it doesn't agree with experiment, it's wrong," Feynman wrote.[7]

You are not a scientist, of course. But you still must take an objective approach in collecting and verifying information. You may begin a story with preliminary assumptions; there's nothing wrong with that. Always be willing, however, to test your assumptions against the evidence you uncover. Every reporter can tell you about a great hunch that never materialized into a great story because the facts did not support it. Do not let your hunches take you places that are unsubstantiated by the facts.

## TAKE THE JOB SERIOUSLY

 or thirty years Edward H. Eulenberg was an editor at Chicago's City News Bureau, where generations of young reporters learned their profession. In *Behind the Front Page*, a history of the bureau, author Arnold Dornfeld said Eulenberg believed that while reporters shouldn't take themselves seriously, they had to take the job seriously. "That was the only way to do it properly. You had to be your own disciplinarian because you worked basically on the street, or away from the eyes of your supervisors."[8]

Eulenberg is credited with establishing the rule that became the bureau's slogan, which continues to motivate the best reporters to this day: *If your mother says she loves you, check it out.*

Bureau editors demanded that reporters ask every question they could think of to get as many details as possible for their stories. They also required that every detail, no matter how small or obvious, be confirmed and then confirmed again. Reporters were forbidden to speculate, assume or suppose. Sources had to be nailed down; information had to be verified.

Pete Weitzel spent 38 years at *The Miami Herald.* He got his basic training as a 17-year-old copy boy/cub reporter at City News when he chased down a police tip about the murder of a one-time lieutenant of gangster Al Capone. Weitzel was in a hospital waiting room when an EMS team brought in the mobster's body, the chest ripped open by shotgun blasts, a large bullet wound in the forehead. Weitzel immediately called his editor to report the killing.

*How do you know he's dead,* the editor demanded.

*I'm looking at him,* Weitzel answered. *He's dead.*

*Are you a goddamned doctor?* the editor asked. *Get him pronounced!*

Weitzel turned to a white-coated man who had just walked into the room. *Are you a doctor? Is he dead? What's your name?*

The doctor pronounced the mobster very dead. This time, Weitzel's editor accepted the report.[9]

Monica Davey worked on her college newspaper, but she had no professional experience before she landed a job at the City News Bureau. She didn't think of herself as naïve, but she quickly learned that nothing she was told was gospel, no matter who the source.[10]

Chicago's daily newspapers routinely ignored what they dismissively called "cheap murders," shootings in bars, domestic killings and the like. City News Bureau reporters, though, covered every homicide no matter how insignificant it might appear. It wasn't easy; the police were notorious in the way they dealt with the bureau's new reporters. The cops often made up stories, piling on elaborate and sometimes disgusting details that gullible rookies swallowed whole. The cops would then sit back and laugh to themselves as the reporter called in the phony information to the bureau.

Davey quickly understood that she needed sharp instincts and had to approach each story with a skeptical eye. Her editors would trip her up when they grilled her about her stories if she didn't, because it was their job to punch holes in stories and to send reporters back to ask the questions they should have asked the first time.

A lot of reporters gloss over the gaps in their stories, Davey says. The City News Bureau didn't allow for that. Reporters who didn't have the answers would always get caught and be sent back to ask the questions again.

The News Bureau trained Davey, now Chicago Bureau Chief of *The New York Times,* to change her way of thinking. She still asks these questions every time she writes a story:

- What hole could my editors poke in my story?
- What am I forgetting?
- Do I have that detail nailed down, or have I made an assumption?
- Have I checked everything out?

Ask yourself these same questions with your stories.

Davey's experience at the bureau taught her that her editors' questions were not personal; they were designed to make her stories better.

"Not knowing something is not the worst thing in the world," Davey says. "I don't mind saying, 'I don't know the answer but I'll find out.' "

## WATCH OUT FOR CYNICISM

Skepticism must be part of every journalist's DNA. The challenge is to prevent skepticism from turning into cynicism, and not all journalists have been able to avoid the trap.

In his 2005 commencement address at Williams College, *New York Times* columnist Thomas Friedman told how a young editor named Nathaniel Nash befriended him in 1982. Nash's colleagues thought his niceness would work against him as a journalist. Friedman said that didn't happen because Nash understood the important distinction between skepticism and cynicism.

"Skepticism is about asking questions, being dubious, being wary, not being gullible, but always being open to being persuaded of a new fact or angle," Friedman told the students at Williams. "Cynicism is about already having the answers—or thinking you do—answers about a person or an event. The skeptic says, 'I don't think that's true; I'm going to check it out.' The cynic says: 'I know that's not true. It couldn't be. I'm going to slam him.' Nathaniel always honored that line."[11]

Nash died in 1996 when he was 44; he was the only American reporter on U. S. Commerce Secretary Ron Brown's plane when it crashed in Croatia.

"Real journalists," Friedman said, "are not those loudmouth talking heads you see on cable television. Real journalists are reporters, like Nathaniel Nash, who go off to uncomfortable and often dangerous places like Croatia and get on a military plane to chase after a visiting dignitary, without giving it a second thought—all to get a few fresh quotes, maybe a scoop, or even just a paragraph of color that no one else had. My prayers were too late for Nathaniel, but he was such a good soul, I am certain that right now he is sitting at God's elbow—taking notes, with skepticism not cynicism."

Be skeptical, but guard against cynicism. Skepticism nurtures good journalism; cynicism can suffocate it. Skepticism lends itself to creativity and imagination; cynicism never does. As Friedman says, we have more than enough cynical journalists in our world to go around. The last thing we need is another one.

## CONCLUSION

The City News Bureau closed on December 31, 2005. Its last dispatch went out just before midnight, with an opening line that echoed the kind of skeptical questions editors had asked young reporters for more than century: "Was the victim killed where his body was found or was he dumped there?"

As this final dispatch shows, you cannot take things at face value. Shannon Harrington, who reported on the Miss Virginia fraud, said good reporters learn that stories that sound too good to be true often aren't true. That's when the skeptical journalist shines a bright light on the situation to distinguish truth from fiction.

Monica Davey says she second-guesses herself on every story until the final hour. Filing a good story means you believe and can verify everything you've written. Your information may seem solid; it may come from official documents and records, the mayor, the police chief, a prosecutor or the pastor of a prominent church. The governor, a congressman, or a White House official may be your source. Or your source might be a beauty pageant contestant, or even your mother.

Trust but verify. Believe what you're told only after you've checked everything out.

## checklist

- **Accuracy is your first responsibility.** Check and double-check your facts.

- **Approach your story like a scientist.** Test your theories and assumptions, and follow the evidence.

- **Don't be overconfident.** You may think you have all the answers, but you probably don't.

- **Use common sense.** If something seems too good to be true, it very well may be false.

- **Review your assumptions.** We go into almost every story with an assumption about how it will turn out. Open your mind to the possibility that things may be different from what you assume.

- **Don't rush to judgment.** Heed your deadline, but be patient as you pursue facts. You *want* to be first, but you *must* be right. It's better to be second and correct with a story than to be first and wrong.

- **Give everyone a fair shake.** Always present someone's best defense in your stories. Let your readers or viewers make up their own minds.

## assignments

1. In his biography *Einstein: His Life and Universe,* Walter Isaacson writes about the seven years Albert Einstein worked as a patent examiner. His boss told him to think that everything the inventors said on their patent applications was incorrect; Einstein's job was to check it all out.[12] Following Einstein's example, review your next story as though you've got it wrong. Look at your story with a skeptical eye and prove to yourself that you've got your story right. Also look for what's missing; figure out what you don't know and what you need to know. Notice things that don't add up, and try to fill in the gaps.

2. Over the coming week, analyze the content of the stories you read in newspapers and online and hear on television and radio. Look for examples that seem to illustrate the difference between healthy skepticism and any instances of journalistic cynicism. Pay particular attention to commentaries in which reporters

express thoughts about issues in the news. How often do you witness a cynical attitude? Are those attitudes backed up by facts, or are they merely opinions?

## notes

1. Interview with Becky Wagoner, February 23, 2009; David Folkenflik, coverage of the Sago mine disaster, *All Things Considered*, January 4, 2006. Available online. http://www.npr.org/ templates/story/story.php?storyId=5126627. Accessed March 30, 2011.

2. Ralph Hanson, comments on the Sago mine disaster, "Living in a Media World" blog. Available online. http://ralphehanson.com/ blog/archive_sago.html. Accessed March 30, 2011.

3. Terence Smith, interview with Jerry Mitchell, *NewsHour*, April 18, 2002; Sherry Ricchiardi, "Out of the Past," *American Journalism Review*, April/May, 2005. Available online. http://www.ajr.org/ Article.asp?id=3852. Accessed April 4, 2011.

4. Brant Houston and Investigative Reporters and Editors, Inc., *The Investigative Reporter's Handbook: A Guide to Documents, Databases and Techniques*, 5th ed., Bedford St. Martin's, 2009.

5. Interview with Shannon Harrington, February 2009.

6. Bill Kovach and Tom Rosenstiel, *The Elements of Journalism: What Newspeople Should Know and the Public Should Expect*, revised ed., Three Rivers Press, 2007.

7. Richard Feynman, *The Character of Physical Law*, MIT Press, 2001, p. 156.

8. Arnold Dornfeld, *Behind the Front Page: The Story of the City News Bureau of Chicago*, Academy Chicago Publishers, 1983.

9. Interview with Pete Weitzel, January 26, 2009.

10. Interview with Monica Davey, January 12, 2009.

11. Thomas Friedman, "Listen to Your Heart," Commencement address at Williams College, June 5, 2005. Available online. http://www.humanity.org/voices/commencements/speeches/ index.php?page=friedman_at_williams. Accessed April 4, 2011.

12. Walter Isaacson, *Einstein: His Life and Universe*, Simon & Schuster, 2007.

# 8

The truth is out there.

FOX MULDER,
FBI AGENT. *THE X-FILES*

# get close to
# your story

erman machine guns spit bullets at Allied soldiers as they jumped
from landing crafts and waded ashore on Omaha Beach in Normandy,
France. Photojournalist Robert Capa was shooting pictures from
one of the boats when a boatswain kicked him out. Capa hit the cold water and
made his way one hundred yards to the beach, where he crawled behind a
burned out amphibious tank for protection.

Capa continued shooting pictures as mortar shells rained down around him.
He tried to load a new roll of film, but his hands were shaking too hard. Live soldiers lay motionless on the beach; only the dead moved as their bodies rolled in
the waves.

Without thinking, Capa ran toward a landing craft that was bringing in medics.
He held his cameras above his head and splashed through the water. Once on
board, he put fresh film in his cameras and shot a last picture of the carnage on
the beach.

Back in England, Capa turned down a plane ride to London where someone
wanted to interview him about his experience as the only war photographer to
make it to the beachhead on D-Day. Instead, he handed over his film and took
the first available boat back to the war. A week later he learned a lab technician

had used too much heat to dry his negatives. Of the 106 pictures he had taken on D-Day, only eight were salvaged.

Capa remained with the Allied forces in Europe during the last year of World War II. In April 1945 he climbed to the fourth floor of a building in Leipzig where five GI's had set up a machine gun to cover an assault on a bridge. Capa walked onto a balcony to take a picture of a young corporal firing the gun. Suddenly, the corporal slumped back into the apartment, shot between the eyes. Capa took another picture, documenting one of the last U. S. combat fatalities of the war in Europe.

In 1954 Capa accepted an assignment from *Life* magazine to cover the French Indochina war. He was in the Red River delta when he stepped on a land mine. His leg was blown to pieces and he was dead by the time he was taken to a medic's tent. He still had his camera with him.

apa's war photos are some of photojournalism's most famous images and established his reputation as one of the great battlefield photographers. His pictures stir us with their images of heroism and horror, but they also inspire us by the courage it took to get them. Capa took his work seriously; he knew there were no shortcuts to covering war or anything else. He knew that if you really want to report a story, you must go to where the story is unfolding. If that requires you to march with troops through rain and mud and snow and cold, that's what you do.

Capa's photographic legacy endures. But an equally important part of his legacy is the credo he lived by: *If your pictures aren't good enough, you aren't close enough.*[1]

Capa was talking specifically about photojournalism, but his advice applies to all forms of journalism. If your stories are not good enough, you probably are not close enough to report them well. Distance prevents you from obtaining on-the-scene color and facts, face-to-face interviews and sensory details that raise a story above the ordinary. You must go out into the world where people live and absorb as much of the richness of their lives as you can. Put yourself in the places where you can see firsthand what is happening. Your stories will become more authoritative, compelling and accurate.

## GOOD REPORTING COMES FROM GETTING OUT THERE

e all want to craft our stories artfully and tell them well. Too many times, though, beginning journalists think that writing counts the most. They haven't learned that the hard job of reporting must take place before they write their first word. Some may even think writing and reporting are the same thing. They're both difficult and important. But they're not the same.

Only when you practice good reporting can you generate good writing. The best reporting comes when you are immersed in the scene, seeing, hearing, smelling and feeling what has happened. The closer you are to the story, the better your reporting will be.

One of the benefits of journalism is the opportunity to go places, see things and meet people. But the best stories will not come to you; they are out there waiting for you to find them.

Meet people face to face. You will never be able to eliminate phone interviews; they save time and help you work efficiently, especially on deadline. But discipline yourself. When possible and practical, conduct interviews in person. You'll learn more when you're face to face with someone than when you're a disembodied voice on the phone. Also, people on your beat must recognize you. If they don't know who you are, they will be less likely to give you the information for your stories. As mentioned in Chapter 5, avoid the lazy trap of e-mail interviews as much as possible. The truth is *out there,* and your job as a journalist is to go out and find it.

The prospect may be scary. Getting to the heart of the scene, approaching people and observing the situation firsthand may be one of the hardest things you learn to do. It's okay to feel daunted; a little bit of fear is healthy. But going out into the world is what the best journalists have always done, even in this wired and computer-dependent age.

## "Shoe leather, shoe leather, shoe leather"

Haynes Johnson understood that the story was *out there.* A Pulitzer Prize winner for his coverage of the civil rights struggle in Selma, Alabama, he later wrote about what he saw as regrettable changes in how many modern journalists go about their jobs.

"In the old days," Johnson wrote, "journalists used to cite approvingly Joseph Pulitzer's famous adage about what formed the essentials of effective journalism: accuracy, accuracy, accuracy . . . I would add another maxim . . . shoe leather, shoe leather, shoe leather. Shoe leather that is worn and expended in the search of the real-life stories of real people. A little bit of knocking on doors is one useful step along that journey. You don't get there by cyberspace alone."[2]

Norman Lockman also understood this. He was the first full-time black reporter hired by the Wilmington, Delaware, *News Journal,* and

Pulitzer-Prize winning columnist Jimmy Breslin once described his job as "walking up tenement steps and ringing doorbells." He lamented how new reporters relied too much on the telephone and did not hit the pavement to sniff out stories. He blamed editors for not encouraging reporters to scarf up the details necessary to turn a routine story into a compelling piece.

"If you get more information, your story is better," Breslin said. "But you've got to get so much in order to know what to leave out."[3]

Getting close to his stories came naturally to Breslin. The weekend after John F. Kennedy was assassinated, the Capitol Rotunda and other major sites in Washington were packed with politicians and lawmakers, statesmen and world leaders. They were also packed with journalists reporting on how Kennedy's death had changed the nation and the world.

Breslin was on the scene, too, but not at the Rotunda or the White House. Instead, he was across the Potomac River at Arlington National Cemetery. That's where he found Clifton Pollard, the man who was digging Kennedy's grave with a backhoe. When the bucket came up with its first scoop of earth, John Metzler, the cemetery's superintendent, studied it.

"'That's nice soil,' Metzler said. 'I'd like to save a little of it,' Pollard said. 'The machine made some tracks in the grass over here and I'd like to sort of fill them in and get some good grass growing there. I'd like to have everything, you know, nice.' "

The nation's top journalists wrote many words from Washington during those dark days; many have been forgotten. Breslin got close to the story in a unique way, and his column is still read today.

he was later a member of *The Boston Globe* team that won a Pulitzer Prize for a series about the city's racial tensions. His final column before his death from Lou Gehrig's disease reminded young journalists about this important lesson: "Good writing cannot be done by phone. It requires being able to scurry around, seeing, tasting and smelling the things you write about from as close as possible without getting mixed up in the story."[4]

These are old pros talking, but their advice still applies today.

Being there matters, says reporter Monica Davey, a national correspondent and the Chicago Bureau Chief for *The New York Times*. You get different material when you're on the ground, she feels. For example, when covering a cop story, you can talk to neighbors and see and hear their reactions, which you'd never get over the phone or from a police report. "It's hard to argue against the beauty of being there," she says.[5]

Lara Logan, the chief foreign correspondent for CBS News, recognized her responsibility to get close to the story when she covered the war in Iraq. She told Jon Stewart of "The Daily Show" that up-close reporting was essential to keeping the American public informed about the war. She lamented that as the war dragged on, some editors were reluctant to air reports from the front lines.

"Tell me the last time you saw the body of a dead American soldier," she said to Stewart. "What does that look like? Who in America knows what that looks like? Because I know what that looks like, and I feel responsible for the fact that no one else does . . . And the soldiers do feel forgotten, they do. No doubt. From Afghanistan to Iraq, they absolutely feel—you know, we may be tired of hearing about this five years later, they still have to go out and do the same job."[6]

Journalists, she said, must live up to their obligation to show what is really happening, something they can do only when they are on the scene.

## Beyond the Internet

Today, many journalists may be tempted to let stories come to them. We can rely on Internet search engines to find lots of material without ever leaving the comfort of our office or home. We can learn about things that happened years ago, yesterday, this morning, or in the last hour. Bloggers trumpet their latest discovery, and Twitter arms us with real-time updates about hometown events and happenings around the world.

All of these are valuable accessories in the journalist's toolkit, but they are not the only tools we should use. Fons Tuinstra, a Danish journalist based in China, has written about how Internet social networks have aided him in covering events all over Asia. However, he also says that journalists must be out on the street if they are to do their job well.

"You do need to meet real people to get an understanding of any society, your own and even more for other societies," he explains. "Fortunately, I got that opportunity in different parts of the world. I believe that because of that experience, I have an advantage in using the online tools that have become so important recently. Whatever you can get from the social networks, for the real thing you need more."[7]

Betsi Freeman, who earned her M. S. in journalism at the University of Illinois in 2009, wrote in an essay that our powers of observation are weakened when we spend hours in front of a computer.[8] She's right. Use digital tools to augment, but not replace, what you can find out on the street. Doing your job well requires you to leave your desk and computer and venture into the world. Online social networks can bring people together, but they can also lead to isolation. Interacting with people face to face, in real time, is essential to doing good journalism.

## MAKING THE MOST OF BEING THERE

**B**arry Bearak's first story as a *New York Times* correspondent in India was about cows in the street. It was, he says now, the biggest cliché imaginable.

Hindus venerate the cow as the giver of life and the symbol of motherhood. It's illegal to kill cows in most of India, and they roam freely in the countryside and cities. In New Delhi alone an estimated 40,000 cows wander the streets, untended and largely unnoticed by most residents.

Bearak thought he was ready for what he would find in India, but he wasn't. The cows were everywhere, and he had never seen anything like it before. All sorts of questions popped into his head: *Do they belong to anyone? What do they eat? What happens if you hit one with your car?*[9]

He began to look for answers and discovered a subculture he had no idea existed. He talked to municipal cowcatchers who were paid $119 a month for rescuing animals that had been hit by vehicles or faced other dangers. The cowcatchers said the old and sick animals didn't put up much of a fight, but the young ones were a different story. A healthy cow required eight men to capture it and the skills of a rodeo cowboy to slip a rope around the cow's head and pull it tight until the animal fell to the ground.

"If you grab the ears and put your hand in its mouth, the cow won't run," a veteran cowcatcher told Bearak. "Then someone's got to hold on to the tail."

Urban cows faced other hazards besides traffic. Many died painful deaths after eating plastic garbage bags scavenged from trash piles. Animal rights groups had begun a campaign to ban the plastic bags, but it was a fight they appeared destined to lose.

The *Times* ran the story, which was then picked up by Indian newspapers that had never written about the problem. It took someone with a fresh perspective to recognize a story that many Indians didn't see, even though it was right in front of them.

India was Bearak's first stint as a foreign correspondent, and he hoped to take a year to prepare for his assignment. That didn't happen, but Bearak said that wasn't necessarily bad. There's a trade-off between having expertise and knowledge and going into a place with a fresh eye. Expertise can pay off when a reporter writes about complex issues, but sometimes it can blind you to obvious stories and even lead to staleness.

## Journalistic attention deficit disorder

A good reporter with a fresh perspective can "see things with the wonderment of someone brand new to a subject," Bearak says of his cow story. "After I had been in India for two or three years, I never, never would have done a story like that."

Sadly, too many journalists have lost the fresh eyes they need to pay close attention to what goes on around them. They talk to the same people, go to the same places, ask the same kinds of questions over and over again. They anticipate nothing out of the ordinary, and they see only the predictable.

Does this sound like anyone you know? Does it sound like you?

It probably describes all of us at some point in our journalism careers. We're on the job, but we don't look beyond the ordinary to capture unexpected stories and the meanings behind them. We take things for granted, either because we've become lazy or self-absorbed with only those subjects that interest us. We have become such creatures of habit that only spectacular events can break through our preoccupation. We fall back on the clichés that have worked in the past without forcing ourselves outside the arbitrary boundaries we've set for ourselves.

Call it *journalistic attention deficit disorder,* a condition in which we hear but don't listen and see but don't observe. We are blind and deaf to the sights and sounds that should astound us. We catch glimpses, but we miss the big picture. We play it safe within the confines of our beats, news organizations and deadlines.

Beware of slipping into this rut. Don't let journalistic attention deficit disorder extinguish your sense of wonderment.

### Be surprised at what you find

How can you recapture a sense of excitement and keep your perspective fresh? The best journalists ask themselves this question every day.

Donald Murray, a writer, editor and teacher of writers, said you fail as a journalist when you stop concentrating and passively let an exciting world pass you by. He believed the best journalists:

- Teach themselves to pay attention to the world in all its details and nuances.
- Notice what is present and what is missing.
- Are alert to what happens as well as what doesn't happen.
- Look for surprises and take delight in the unexpected.[10]

Exercising these traits, Murray said, enables you capture the powerful details that will serve as the building blocks for your stories.

Murray confessed that he thought of himself as a poet and novelist when he first went to work at the *Boston Herald,* more interested in style and theory than delivering information clearly and gracefully. As he learned the craft of journalism, though, he discovered what he called a "new love" for specific, meaningful details. He sought out such details everywhere he went, knowing that revealing facts would improve his work.

His breakthrough came when he arrived at a hotel where a man threatened to jump from a ledge. The lead reporter went to the man's hotel room, while Murray, who was the backup reporter on the story, headed to the street below. Immersed in a bloodthirsty crowd yelling "Jump! Jump! Jump!" Murray scribbled notes, getting quotes and descriptions and capturing the crowd's anger when it became clear the man would not commit suicide.

From that point on, he said, he tried to "get out of the way of the information, to construct my stories with specific information."

Years later, in a brief memo to a new features reporter, Murray summarized the challenge all journalists face as they go about the daily work of gathering information they need for their stories:

> Your ability to write well is based on your ability to see well. And we want you on the street, and discovering what is extraordinary in what has become ordinary for the rest of us.
>
> We want to know what you catch out of the corner of your eye, what you overhear being said and not said, what you discover when you observe our world from your own point of view. We hope you'll continue to be surprised at what you find and that you'll continue to surprise us and our readers.[11]

You cannot write from nothing, Murray said. Good writing is derived from the building blocks of accurate, revealing details. Finding those details requires that you pay attention to the world and remain alert to the possibilities around you. Don't let your senses go dull.

Instead, use all of your senses: sight and hearing, certainly, but also touch, smell and taste. Describe the sun setting over a Midwest cornfield or the sounds of an auto factory on its last day of operation. How do you describe the feel of a saw as it cuts through timber, the aroma of a bakery or the peaty taste of real Scotch whisky?

## Concentration and analysis

Paying attention is more than taking copious notes. Good observation, William Ruehlmann says, requires two things: concentration and analysis. Journalists are observers by occupation and always on the job; everything you encounter is a potential story. But you must know what to make of the material once you find it. As you conscientiously record your observations, also apply your intellect to what you've learned, asking what a detail means and where it will lead you in your reporting. Failure to do so, Ruehlmann writes in *Stalking the Feature Story,* reduces your observations to "cataloging reality instead of revealing it."[12] You've collected the data, now what does it signify?

Think of your brain as a muscle, Thomas Kunkel says, that gets stronger the more you use it. When he was dean of the College of Journalism at the University of Maryland, Kunkel routinely sent students in his news feature writing class out for a lap around the campus mall to write down everything they had never noticed before. Each time, the students came back with dozens of great story ideas, a testament to their powers of observation and analysis.

In a column for *American Journalism Review,* Kunkel praised his students for opening his eyes. "I've been on campus nearly eight years, yet I learned so much from your stories about this place that you made me feel I'd scarcely been paying attention. That's what good feature writers do."[13]

It all begins with the reporting, the physical act of going out to see and hear what's happening. Nothing—not even raw talent—can substitute for reporting. Distinguish yourself by aggressively applying your senses to your craft, Kunkel said. "Young reporters often feel that story generation is their biggest challenge. But coming up with a good idea for a news feature doesn't take magic. It takes paying attention."

Your job is to carefully listen, see, feel, taste and touch so you can convey those experiences to your readers and viewers. Then exercise your brain muscle to detect patterns, connect the dots, offer explanations and make sense of a world that is complicated and often confusing. To do that you must get out of your box and rise above the madness of hourly, daily or weekly journalism to see the looming stories that others miss.

Go into the weeds and get lost on the side roads. See what is present and notice what is missing. Hear the noises and the voices, but pay attention to the silences and to the things left unsaid. Don't let amazing stories escape because you aren't paying attention.

### Keep your antennae up

You can pay attention in many different ways.

*New York Times* investigative reporter Walt Bogdanich read about a rash of deaths in Panama, all caused by cold medicine that had been supposedly accidentally poisoned. He didn't understand how something like that could be an accident. His curiosity led to a series about how toxins from China got into consumer goods that were sold on the world market; the series won the 2008 Pulitzer Prize for investigative reporting.[14]

Maurice Possley and Steve Mills of the *Chicago Tribune* were intrigued by something they *didn't* see when they investigated an execution in Texas. Carlos DeLuna was arrested for the murder of a female gas station attendant less than an hour after she was stabbed to death. Although he identified another man as the killer, DeLuna was quickly convicted of capital murder and eventually executed by lethal injection.

Years later Possley and Mills got a tip that the man DeLuna initially identified was indeed the killer. In the course of their reporting, they saw something that should have made an impression on authorities at the scene of the crime but didn't.

The victim had been stabbed multiple times, and pictures from the gas station showed a grisly, bloody scene. But the pictures police took of DeLuna immediately after his arrest offered contradictory evidence.

"You see the picture of him and there's no blood . . . on this guy forty-five minutes after the crime," Possley says now. "There were other factors, but that was the thing for me."[15]

Possley and Mills revealed that DeLuna's case was marred by questionable eyewitness accounts and sloppy police work. They also showed that investigators failed to pursue the man identified by DeLuna even though he bragged to family and friends that he was the killer.

Dana Priest of *The Washington Post* paid attention to a tip from someone she didn't know about how injured Marines and soldiers and their family members were mistreated at Walter Reed Army Medical Center. Priest told the Poynter Institute's Al Tompkins that she met with the caller, and she and reporter Anne Hull began an investigation that documented how the hospital systematically mistreated and neglected soldiers who had been wounded in Iraq and Afghanistan. Their series won a Pulitzer Prize for public service in 2008.[16]

Poldek Pfefferberg, a Polish Jew, tried for 30 years to interest people in the story of a man who had saved him from extermination by the Nazis during World War II. No one really listened until an Australian writer named Thomas Keneally came into his shop to buy a new briefcase. Keneally paid attention and wrote about Pfefferberg's savior, whose name was Oscar Schindler, the privileged German businessman who bought a factory and saved its Jewish slave workers from death. The result was Keneally's book, *Schindler's Ark,* a best seller that was later adapted for film as *Schindler's List* and won an Academy Award for best picture.[17]

Beth Macy won state and national awards for stories in *The Roanoke Times* about the lives and problems of the elderly, unwed teenage mothers and immigrants. Her advice for other journalists is to keep your antennae up and look for things that surprise and astonish you. Pay special attention to what moves you emotionally.

"If it's empathy for the underdog, so be it. . . . It's our job to convince our subjects that we're in it for the long haul—whether it means planting ourselves in the middle of a living-room floor so we can finally make eye contact with a battered African refugee, or joining a group of migrant guest workers in the predawn as they set out on a four-day journey home to Mexico.

"It's our job to nurture our inner-tugs and goose bumps, and to know without a doubt: These are *my* stories, the stories that *I* was born to tell."[18]

## CONCLUSION

he best reporters—beginners and veterans alike—accept no substitute for walking up tenement steps and knocking on doors, or driving to the scene of an event and talking to people. There's no substitute for shoe leather, legwork and being there. In an era when reporters are expected to document stories through audio and video, the importance of being engaged and on the scene becomes even more important. If you miss images or sounds when they occur, they are gone for good.

The lesson of Robert Capa applies to everything you do as a journalist: If your stories aren't good enough, you probably aren't close enough. The truth is out there, but you have to look for it.

Pay attention to the world you find. Do it well, and you will find things that will surprise you and your audience. Do it well, and you will discover the extraordinary in life that others miss.

What stories were you born to tell?

## checklist

- **Get up and go.** Some stories may come to you, but the best ones will be those you find for yourself.
- **Set a goal of spending at least half of your workday on the street.** You won't do all your work in the field, but the more you are out there the richer your stories will be.
- **Talk to people in person whenever you can.** It takes more time, and it may not always be possible when you're working on a tight deadline. Use the phone when necessary and e-mail only sparingly.
- **Use the Internet to supplement, not replace, your on-the-scene reporting.** You can learn a lot of valuable information in cyberspace, but you should never spend all of your reporting time there.
- **Walk to places.** Or take the bus. Eat lunch and drink coffee at local hot spots. Pay attention to the people around you and find out what's on their minds.
- **Open your eyes.** Note the surroundings of the people you talk to. What's on the desk and the walls in the school superintendent's office? What's in the refrigerator of the welfare mother trying to make ends meet for her children? What kind of books and magazines does the candidate for political office keep in his home?
- **Open your ears.** What do you hear in the schoolyard and the hall as you report on what goes on in a high school classroom? Are people waiting for news about an injured friend or relative in a hospital emergency room talkative, or are they quiet and reflective?

■ **Change your habits.** Take a different route to work or school. Note things you've never seen before. Break the habits that can blind you to the exceptional things happening around you.

■ **Challenge your assumptions.** You may think you know what life is like in a particular part of your community. Make a list of things and attitudes you expect to encounter in a given neighborhood. Then go there and see if your expectations match reality.

■ **Do new things.** Visit places you've never been and meet new people. Get lost and stop for directions. You never know what you'll discover when you ask for help.

## assignments

1. Team up with a partner to report a story about an event in your coverage area and split the responsibilities. One of you works the story by phone or by computer. The other goes to the scene and gathers firsthand information and details. The on-the-scene reporter should knock on doors, talk to people and seek out eyewitnesses. When both of you are finished writing your stories, compare what each of you came up with in your reporting.

    a. What elements did the on-the-scene reporter develop that the office reporter could not?

    b. Did the office reporter find out facts that the on-the-scene reporter could not?

    c. Who had richer material for the final story?

    d. Who wrote the strongest and most complete story?

2. Complete the exercise that Thomas Kunkel assigned his students at the University of Maryland. Spend an hour wandering your campus or another familiar public area with your notebook and camera. Note things that you've never really seen before, things that are simply different, interesting or surprising. How many new impressions can you come away with? How many could you turn into a story? What does this exercise tell you about your powers of observation when you're operating in your normal mode? What can you do differently to become more attentive to your surroundings and the people around you?

**notes**

1. Alex Kershaw, *Blood and Champagne: The Life and Times of Robert Capa*, St. Martin's, 2003, p. 164.

2. Haynes Johnson, *Nieman Reports,* summer 1995.

3. David Nyhan, "Jimmy Breslin: The Bard of Queens," *Washington Journalism Review,* October 1986; Jimmy Breslin, "Digging JFK Grave Was His Honor." *New York Herald Tribune,* November 1963. Available online. www.arlingtoncemetery.net/digging-grave-an-honor.htm. Accessed April 1, 2011.

4. Tom Long, "Norman Lockman, 66; Part of Pulitzer-winning Effort." *Boston Globe,* April 20, 2005. Available online. www.boston.com/news/globe/obituaries/articles/2005/04/20/norman_lockman_66_part_of_pulitzer_winning_effort/. Accessed April 4, 2011.

5. Interview with Monica Davey, January 12, 2009.

6. Lara Logan, interview on *The Daily Show with Jon Stewart,* Comedy Central, June 17, 2008. Available online. www.thedailyshow.com/watch/tue-june-17-2008/lara-logan. Accessed April 4, 2011.

7. Fons Tuinstra, e-mail exchange, December 7, 2008.

8. Betsi Freeman wrote her essay for the fall 2008 semester of Journalism 400, the introductory reporting class for journalism students at the University of Illinois.

9. Interview with Barry Bearak, February 13, 2009; Barry Bearak, "Sacred Cows Are Wily Too; Just Try Catching One," *New York Times,* October 21, 1998.

10. Donald M. Murray, *Writing to Deadline: The Journalist at Work,* Heinemann, 2000, pp. 4–6.

11. Donald M. Murray, "Memo to a New Feature Writer," in *The Complete Book of Feature Writing,* ed. Leonard Witt, Writer's Digest Books, 1991, p. 15.

12. William Ruehlmann, *Stalking the Feature Story,* Vintage Books, 1977.

13. Thomas Kunkel, "Dear JOUR371," *American Journalism Review,* February/March 2005.

14. Steve Myers, "Avoid Conventional Wisdom and Uncover Investigative Gems." Poynter.org, June 6, 2008. Available online. www.poynter.org/content/content_view.asp?id=144815. Accessed April 4, 2011.

15. Interview with Maurice Possley, January 24, 2009; Maurice Possley and Steve Mills, "Did This Man Die . . . for This Man's Crime?" *Chicago Tribune,* June 25, 26, 27, 2006.

16. Al Tompkins, interview with Dana Priest, in *Best Newspaper Writing,* CQ Press, 2009.

17. Poldak Pfefferberg, Schindler Survivors website. www.auschwitz.dk/Panzuck/id4.htm. Accessed April 1, 2011.

18. Interview with Beth Macy, August 28, 2008; Beth Macy, "Notice What You Notice," *American Journalism Review,* August/September 2008.

First you have to know the subject. Then you have to know how to write. Both take a lifetime to learn.

ERNEST HEMINGWAY,
"OLD NEWSMAN WRITES:
A LETTER FROM CUBA," 1934

# know your place

Tom and Pat Gish had nearly twenty years of news experience between them when they bought *The Mountain Eagle,* a weekly paper in eastern Kentucky's Letcher County. The couple had met at the University of Kentucky, and after graduation Pat became a reporter for the *Lexington Leader* and Tom worked for United Press International and covered politics and government in Frankfort, Kentucky's capital. They married, started a family and dreamed of owning their own newspaper.

Tom had grown up in a Letcher County coal camp and read *The Mountain Eagle* as a child. A typical county weekly, it avoided hard reporting and controversies; its motto was "A Friendly Non-Partisan Weekly Newspaper Published Every Thursday."

Tom and Pat changed all that. They discovered the *Eagle*'s motto had once been "It Screams!" and restored it to the masthead, launching a half-century of reporting that may be unequaled in the annals of small-town weeklies. When the worst floods in a generation devastated the region, they put out two issues that matched the coverage by the Lexington and Louisville papers. They continued to report on the disaster after the dailies had moved on to other stories.

They challenged secrecy and corruption in local government and were among the first to write about environmental problems caused by strip mining. They told readers about deplorable conditions in local schools and about communities that didn't have adequate public water or sewage services. They wrote about unsafe mines and black lung disease and covered how impoverished citizens in the hollows and mountains of eastern Kentucky coped with hunger and inadequate health care. They criticized banks that charged higher interest rates for mortgages than those in other parts of the state, and they reported how coal company trucks wrecked mountain roads. They also kept an eye on how the timber, natural gas and oil industries treated the environment.

The Gishes developed enemies. Government agencies declared their offices and meetings off limits to *Eagle* reporters. The school board chairman told teachers and parents to boycott the paper; car dealers and bankers pulled ads. The electric company urged businesses to cancel advertising and subscriptions because the publishers were communists. Tom's father helped feed the Gish family, pay their light bills and keep the paper alive.

Early one morning, someone threw a firebomb through a window and destroyed the newspaper office. Tom and Pat set up shop in their living room and on their front porch to publish the next issue of the *Eagle*. Its new motto: "It Still Screams!"

More than four decades later, the Gishes marveled at what they did not know when they started.

"We didn't know that the coal economy was falling apart," they wrote in a 2000 essay about their work. "We didn't know that one of every two mountain adults couldn't read or write. We didn't know that tens of thousands had been plunged into the extremes of poverty, with children and adults suffering from hunger and some dying of starvation."[1]

But they did learn, and they came to understand the place they called home and the people who lived there. They treasured the work of writers who chronicled the everyday happenings of their communities; the births, deaths, marriages, graduations and homecomings, even the bounty of the area's vegetable gardens. Years later some residents still opposed how the *Eagle* covered the news, but others depended on it and complained if the paper didn't send a reporter to a meeting.

"Don't think you know more than the people who read the *Eagle* because you don't," Tom told new reporters. "*Eagle* subscribers are as smart as anybody in the country."

Big stories were important, but Tom and Pat required reporters who came from outside the region to learn as much as they could about the daily life of Letcher County first. Often that meant going to square dances and other local events; it was the only way they would get to know the place they were covering.

"To really connect with *Eagle* readers and understand them and their region," a former staffer wrote later, "I also needed to write about the school board and the fiscal court and to get to know as many people as possible, even if I never used them in a story.

"That local credibility enabled the *Eagle* and its reporters to scream to the nation."[2]

**Y**ou may have a hard time imagining yourself covering a place the way the Gishes covered their part of Kentucky. Maybe you grew up in one place and went to school somewhere else, and now you're about to enter an especially transient profession. You may long to work in a big city like Chicago or New York, but it's more likely you'll start out at a news operation in a small or medium-sized community.

No matter where you start out as a journalist or where you end up, it's important to develop an intimate knowledge of each community you write about. You need to learn the geography, of course, but there's more to it than that. You must also become familiar with the inner workings of the people who live there. Learn what makes them tick, what they care about and what motivates them in their daily lives.

You can't do this on the fly. It requires discipline, a dedicated approach, respect and even something akin to affection for the community. You must actually care about what happens to the place and its people if you are to report honestly and compassionately.

This may sound contrary to what you've been told about how to conduct yourself as a journalist. You've probably been drilled to avoid conflicts of interest, or even the appearance of conflicts that could cause readers to question your personal agenda in reporting a story. But there is a difference between avoiding a conflict of interest and taking an active interest in the community you cover. Avoiding a conflict of interest means you shouldn't wear political buttons, display bumper sticks, sign political petitions, march in public demonstrations or participate in social actions that might compromise your ability to report, edit or photograph a story fairly. This also applies to your posts on social networks such as Facebook or Twitter. These measures preserve your impartiality and protect your credibility, but they don't require you to be indifferent to or prevent you from taking an active interest in the places you cover. Be engaged in the life of your community. Go to the places where people live, work and play, where they go to school and where they make decisions about governing their lives.

Your job as a journalist is to keep your community informed about what is going on and bring context to events. This requires intimate knowledge of the places you serve and represent, which can only happen if you are truly a part of the community. To make your presence felt, you must actually be present. You cannot reflect on what you have not seen firsthand. To know—to understand deeply—the place you serve, you must live in it wholeheartedly.

You may even need to love it, though that does not allow you to turn a blind eye to its faults. In fact, the more you become a part of your place, the more credibility you will have when, like Tom and Pat Gish and *The Mountain Eagle,* you point out the community's flaws and shortcomings.

## STRENGTHENING YOUR RELATIONSHIP WITH YOUR COMMUNITY

As managing editor of *The Miami Herald,* Pete Weitzel oversaw the development of the country's first daily suburban tabloid supplement as well as the creation of *El Herald,* the first foreign-language edition published daily with a U. S. newspaper. He understood how critical it is for a news organization to gain the trust and respect of its readers, thus he became an advocate for public journalism, also known as civic journalism, a movement that encourages news organizations to help build the civic life of the communities they serve.

Unfortunately, traditional news organizations may not really reflect their communities. Newsrooms may not be as diverse as their communities in terms of race, ethnicity and gender, and recent job cutbacks threaten to make the situation even more imbalanced. Some reporters may believe they need to distance themselves from the civic activities of their community, and thus may share few common experiences with ordinary citizens. They might reside in the community, but not see themselves as a part of its civic life.

As an advocate of public journalism, Weitzel asked hard questions to challenge journalists to think more broadly about their relationship with their communities. Ask yourself the same questions.

- Do you accurately reflect your place? Do you understand the people and the issues that are important to them?
- Do your stories feel like they come from the places where your readers live? Is there a sense of *here* in your stories, a sense that they come only from your particular place and time?
- Do you understand and report on the priorities your community has set for itself?
- Do you acknowledge that your community is not singular but plural, that multiple communities exist? Does your journalism serve as a bridge to help different communities understand each other? Do you offer insights that help your readers and viewers

appreciate the similarities and the differences between those distinct communities?

■ Are you comprehensive in your reporting? Do your stories provide a proper context to keep things in perspective?

■ Do your stories get people talking, or do they block conversations?[3]

To understand what makes one place different from another, Weitzel says, take the time to listen to people and learn what is important to them. Build relationships with official sources as well as ordinary citizens who may have no authority but often have the deepest insight into what local events mean. Everything depends on the relationships you form with individuals in the community and how well you listen to what they tell you. The stronger the relationship, the greater the trust between you and the community, all of which helps make your reporting more influential.

As a journalist, you should seek answers and present them in ways that explain and describe what has happened, along with the consequences of an event and possible alternatives. You can do this effectively only when you have taken the time to understand the place you serve.

## Be on the scene

Chapter 8 talked about the importance of being there for getting the details of a story. Unfortunately, the number of professional journalists on the streets has declined, even as the demand for news and information has grown. This pattern is particularly prevalent at newspapers, where staff cuts have drastically reduced the number of reporters on the street to find out what's on people's minds.

Michael Bugeja, the director of the Greenlee School of Journalism and Communication at Iowa State University, says newspapers created a mess for themselves by de-emphasizing the places they purport to serve. Newspapers, he wrote in *Editor & Publisher,* have an "outdoor history" ranging from paperboys and newsstand street sales to reporters on the beat. Now, instead of capitalizing on what had been their strength, many papers have pulled their forces indoors and given them new assignments that reduce their effectiveness.

The lack of professional journalists on the street has paved the way for the citizen journalists, says Bugeja. "They were on the scene. We weren't," he wrote. "Why would any high school student ever pick up a newspaper rather than an iPod when he or she has never seen a reporter on the beat in the schools? Why would anybody trust a newspaper whose reporters they seldom see? It's as simple as that."[4]

In recent years some news organizations have tried to correct the trend through "hyper-local" coverage, using correspondents, bloggers and some full-time staffers to report on local events.

Online start-ups are attempting to fill in the gaps of local news coverage. Patch.com, for instance, has an ambitious plan to provide intensive local coverage for communities around the country that are underserved by news media and whose residents lack information about government, schools and business. EveryBlock started in 2007 as an online operation providing civic information about local neighborhoods in Chicago. By March 2010 it had created sites for 16 U. S. cities, including New York, Seattle and San Francisco. Each site links to news articles and posts from local bloggers, along with data feeds from city governments, with crime reports, restaurant inspections, and notices of road construction and film shoots.

You may find yourself working for one of these non-traditional organizations, which will still require you to be familiar with every street on your beat. The more deeply you understand the place you cover, the greater the chance of your success.

## Get to know your community and the people who live in it

What can you do to prepare yourself to cover a new place?

▪ Use your news organization's archives and the public library to research your community. Then get out there to explore what it's really like. Walk the neighborhoods; visit schools, businesses and government offices; go to the parks and community centers. Soon you'll know where people congregate and what kinds of activities define the area.

▪ Personal contact can't be beat. Meet people in person rather than talking over the phone. If people on your beat don't recognize you, you'll never get the information you need to write compelling stories.

▪ Official sources from the government, police agencies, business and education are important, but don't forget about assistants, staff, custodians and other behind-the-scenes people. They may know more about what's going on than the authorities.

▪ Talk to as many "real" people—ordinary citizens in neighborhood and civic organizations—as you can to find out what's on their minds. Take into consideration the lessons of the previous chapters about asking good questions and listening carefully.

Don't pretend to know more than you do. People will respect your candor, and as your knowledge grows they'll respect your professionalism.

Develop a source book as you meet people. Collect business cards and record names, phone numbers and e-mail addresses. Keep notes and write down personal information about the people you meet.

Find out where public records are kept in your community, and learn about your state's freedom of information laws. It's better to know what your rights are before you run into roadblocks from officials who may not want to turn over public documents and records.

Talk to the person who covered the community before you. Ask for advice and tips. Which sources were helpful and trustworthy, and who were the difficult ones?

Challenge yourself and set goals. For example, tell yourself that you will meet one new person every day for two weeks.

Look for the enterprise stories that aren't tied to planned events but grow out of tips gathered from the people you talk to.

## KEEP AN EYE ON THE WORLD

The journalist's primary role is to give citizens news and information they need to make wise political, economic and social decisions that will affect their lives and communities. This is an awesome obligation, but don't become so focused on local events that you ignore what's happening in other parts of the world. What happens around the world affects people in every local community.

Unfortunately, many young adults in the United States have little knowledge about what happens in other countries. A 2006 National Geographic–Roper Public Affairs survey revealed that 63 percent of Americans ages 18 to 24 could not find Iraq or Saudi Arabia on a map, and three-quarters could not find Iran or Israel. Five years after the United States' invasion of Afghanistan, nearly 90 percent could not locate that country. More than half did not know that Sudan and Rwanda are in Africa, and 70 percent could not find North Korea.[5]

Ted Gup, chair of the journalism department at Emerson College, quizzed his journalism students on current events when he taught at Case Western Reserve University. He was chagrined by what they didn't know about national and international events and saw their ignorance as a serious threat to society. How, he wondered, could one reconcile the students' lack of knowledge with the idea that they were part of the Internet information age? Unless steps are taken to erase the real information gap, he said, an entire generation will be "left behind and left out."[6]

"No man is an island, entire of itself," the poet John Donne wrote in his famous "Meditation XVII." What Donne affirmed in the seventeenth century holds even truer today. Despite all its governments, religions, ethnicities and races, the world is more connected than ever, even though many insist on remaining apart. As a citizen and a journalist, you must recognize the dangers this form of isolationism creates for our society. What happens in your community can affect the rest of the nation and the world; and what happens elsewhere affects the place where you live. The burning of a Quran by a Florida preacher provoked a mob to kill United Nations aid workers in Afghanistan. A nuclear disaster in Japan prompted U.S. congressional hearings about the safety of nuclear plants in the United States.

To be responsible as both a journalist and a citizen, you must comprehend what's going on in the rest of the world. Isolation is not an option in today's increasingly global and interconnected society.

Get off your island. There's too much going on in the world that you need to know about.

## CONCLUSION

Tom Gish died November 21, 2008, of kidney and heart problems. Pat Gish remains the publisher of *The Mountain Eagle,* though she no longer plays a role in its day-to-day operations.

The *Eagle* still screams, both on its masthead and in its pages. Ben Gish, Tom and Pat's oldest child, is now the editor. He was six weeks old when his parents moved to Letcher County, and he began working at the paper when he was five. By the time he was 12 he was running the offset press. Growing up, he hated the newspaper business because he worked there so much.

Yet he went to the University of Kentucky like his parents and studied journalism. After graduation he planned to apply for a job at a daily paper, but the *Eagle* was down a couple of reporters. He started as a reporter in January 1980 and never went anywhere else.

Ben Gish says his parents sometimes doubted whether staying in Letcher County was the right thing to do, but he and his siblings always assured them it was.

Some things have changed. Multinational corporations now own the coal mines and the car dealers that once boycotted the paper have gone out of business. But Ben Gish says a lot of the big issues remain the same: the pervasiveness of poverty and the environmental destruction caused by the natural gas and extraction industries.

Now in his fifties, Gish says he's still learning about Letcher County and its people. He took his mother to a funeral at the Baptist Church, and Masons performed the rites. It was the first time Gish had seen a Masonic ceremony; as a journalist, he marveled at what he saw and heard.

"How could you be a reporter and editor if you weren't able to take all that in?" he asked.

Gish says two lessons from his parents stand out. The first was how hard they worked at getting a wedding announcement or family reunion story into the paper. They treated that kind of news with as much respect as they did any big story. The second: Never sell out.

"I can remember being in grade school and our cars had holes in the floorboard," he says. "We were poor because my parents believed in doing the right thing."[7]

He and the *Eagle* still try to do that.

## checklist

▪ **Learn your territory.** Visit as many places as you can. Drop into barber shops and hair salons. Go to various houses of worship, cafes and coffee shops. Don't forget about bars and taverns.

▪ **Do your research.** Read up on the history of your community. Check your organization's online database or library. Go to the public library and get to know the people who work there. They want to get information out to the public just like you do.

▪ **Get to know the people.** Look for the individuals in your community who are tuned into the neighborhood network. Talk to them and hear what they have to say. Seek out diversity.

▪ **Talk to your predecessor.** She covered the beat or the community for umpteen years and is a valuable resource. Ask for advice and tips.

▪ **Read bulletin boards.** Look at classified ads in local newspapers. Check out personal notices. Read the legal ads. See what's posted on Craig's List. They can give you ideas for stories and also help you discover interesting tidbits about the area.

▪ **Show respect.** The people of your community may be smarter than you are. Learn from them.

## assignments

1. Be diligent in finding out what's going on in the rest of the world. Your local newspaper may not include international coverage. The network and cable news shows have also cut back their foreign reporting, though CNN still has an international presence. NPR also devotes significant time to international stories.

2. Rate your general knowledge of the world on a scale from 1 to 10, with 1 being low and 10 being expert. Then choose a news source you haven't read before that includes strong international coverage (such as the BBC, *The New York Times* or *The Economist*). Read it every day for a week. Then consider these questions:

   - How would you rate your world knowledge now?
   - Is there an area of the world you now know more about?
   - Are you seeing a change in what you notice when you read your regular news sources?

## notes

1. Tom Gish and Pat Gish, essay in *The Business of Journalism: 10 Leading Reporters and Editors on the Perils and Pitfalls of the Press,* ed. William Serrin, New Press, 2000. Excerpts available online at *The Rural Blog.* http://irjci.blogspot.com/2008/11/tom-gish-inspirational-rural-editor.html. Accessed April 5, 2011.

2. "Tom Gish, Newspaperman" and "Tom Gish Remembered," *The Mountain Eagle,* November 26, 2008; R. G. Dunlap, "Crusading publisher Tom Gish dies at 82," *The Courier-Journal,* November 22, 2008.

3. Interview with Pete Weitzel, January 26, 2009.

4. Michael Bugeja, "The Internet Trap," *Editor & Publisher,* May 2005; "The Fundamental Truths of Our Business," *Editor & Publisher,* August 2007.

5. "Final Report: The National Geographic/Roper Public Affairs 2006 Geographic Literacy Study." 2006. Available online. http://www.nationalgeographic.com/roper2006/pdf/FINALReport2006GeogLitsurvey.pdf. Accessed April 5, 2011.

6. Ted Gup, "So Much for the Information Age," *The Chronicle of Higher Education,* April 11, 2008.

7. Interview with Ben Gish, February 15, 2009.

# 10

*Luck favors the prepared.*

LOUIS PASTEUR

# prepare yourself
# for the unexpected

A steady rain began on Halloween afternoon in Roanoke, Virginia, and parents vainly tried to keep their youngsters dry as they went trick-or-treating. Showers continued the next day and through the weekend. The National Weather Service issued a flood watch, something residents expected during heavy rains because of the city's location in a narrow valley beside the Roanoke River.

Editors and reporters at *The Roanoke Times* remained on alert over the weekend, but only minor problems occurred, and by Monday they turned their attention to other matters. Tuesday was Election Day in Virginia, one with historic implications. Democratic State Senator Douglas Wilder was running a strong race for lieutenant governor. If he won, he would be the first African American elected to statewide office in the South in the twentieth century.

The *Times* had a comprehensive plan for covering the election, but its enthusiasm was tempered by other distractions. A recently converted press was underperforming, often running hours behind schedule and causing late deliveries. Photographs were blurry, and smudges were common. Angry readers threatened

97

to cancel subscriptions, and advertisers complained that they couldn't rely on the paper to deliver timely, high-quality ads to potential customers.

The press problems cascaded into the newsroom. Editors imposed earlier deadlines, which meant that many late-breaking stories made it into the paper a day later than normal. The local television news teams took advantage of the situation and used their late-night and early-morning shows to report stories missing from the newspaper. They also delighted in talking about the paper's press problems and un-happy readers. The *Times'* newsroom was frustrated and embarrassed.

The news department was coping with another problem as well. Work crews had torn out walls, ripped up floors and pulled down ceiling tiles for a major reno-vation. Desks were shoved together, with reporters and editors almost sitting on top of one another. A plastic sheet draped down the middle of the newsroom was the only barrier between the reporters and the chaos of the construction area.

By the Monday after Halloween, conditions in the newsroom had deterio-rated even more. The ceiling began to leak. Trashcans collected rainwater that dripped—and sometimes poured—onto desktops and floors. Tempers were short. The mood was sour.

Then all hell broke loose.

A low-pressure system settled over the valley while the remnants of a Gulf Coast hurricane gathered strength and moved into the area. The two systems col-lided, and the heavens opened up.

Seven inches of rain poured down within hours. Ground saturated by the weekend rains could not absorb the new precipitation. A normally peaceful creek flooded homes in one part of the city, forcing residents to scramble onto rooftops. Some said they could hear dogs, leashed on porches, barking and struggling as they drowned. People in one neighborhood were trapped in an attic and pounded on the roof to be rescued. Two women drowned on the second floors of their homes.

A woman's car stalled in floodwater as she tried to cross a bridge over another creek. She got her ten-year-old grandson and three-year-old granddaughter out, but all three were swept away. The girl was found hours later, wearing a yellow rain-coat, on an island in the creek. Her grandmother and brother had drowned.

A torrent of water dragged a paramedic a hundred yards down a swollen creek. He clung to a tree for five hours until the waters receded.

Another creek washed away a neighborhood grocery store. Its employees climbed to the roof and were lifted to safety by a television news helicopter as the building collapsed. Footage of the dramatic rescue ran repeatedly over the next few weeks.

Five feet of water flooded downtown businesses and covered parked cars and trucks. People navigated some streets by boat.

A three-story apartment complex along the Roanoke River was half sub-merged. The city's largest hospital, just yards from the river, lost power in its 15-story west wing. Nurses used candles and flashlights to maneuver in the dark.

The waters dislodged mobile homes and sent them floating downstream. Truck trailers were lifted from their berths in industrial parks and carried hundreds of yards.

The flood of November 4, 1985, was the worst ever to hit Roanoke, and it came with no warning.

An adrenaline rush hit reporters in the Roanoke newsroom as the scope of the flood became apparent; tempers cooled and bad moods vanished. The election was important, but the flood was an emergency. The newsroom had a natural disaster on its hands; people were dying and others were at risk. Plans had to change fast.

The police radios in the newsroom crackled with the frantic voices of dispatchers delivering nonstop updates and alerts. Sirens of emergency response vehicles echoed throughout the valley. Chaos engulfed the region.

This story could not be reported by phone. Teams of reporters and photographers fanned out to all corners of the valley.

While reporters and editors raced to cover the unfolding disaster, the employees who remained at the downtown office had other worries. The pressroom crews and production workers watched nervously as the water surged steadily toward their building, swallowing cars and trucks in its path. If it reached the building, the ground-floor pressroom would be flooded, which meant another press in another city would have to print the paper. Deadlines would have to be moved up even earlier, resulting in less thorough coverage. The newsroom dreaded another blow to its professional dignity.

The water finally stopped just yards from the pressroom. Everyone breathed a sigh of relief. The next day's paper would be published in-house, with presses that, if not always reliable, were at least its own.

Additional copy editors were called in to handle the heavy load of news stories. Editors increased the number of pages in the next day's paper as well as the numbers of papers to be printed. The *Times*'s more than 120,000 subscribers would not accept any excuses for a substandard edition featuring such a major news story.

The flood dominated Tuesday's paper, along with an appropriate acknowledgement of Election Day. Wednesday's front page covered the flood and the election; Wilder won, as did his running mates for governor and attorney general. Again, editors increased the size of the paper and the number of copies that were printed. News staffers were tired, but their adrenaline sustained them. A week after the flood, the paper published a 10-page special section that documented the flood in story and pictures. Thirty-four reporters and nine photographers contributed to the project, and all had worked virtually around the clock since the first reports of flooding came in.

They were doing what they were supposed to do as journalists, and there is no better feeling than that.[1]

ournalists must always be prepared for the unexpected. Killer flashfloods are rare, but you will need to adapt to changing conditions just about every working day. Unanticipated events will override your plans, and you must confront the new situation immediately and confidently. Not every day will be chaos, but every day will contain constant interruptions and necessary course corrections. You must be ready to move in an entirely different direction on a moment's notice.

Even coverage for annual and organized events requires planning. Dwayne Yancey, who coordinated the *Times*'s election coverage for a dozen years, put together meticulous plans for the newsroom to cover each event. Yancey spelled out in great detail assignments for individual reporters and editors even though he knew that elections, like everything else in life, have a way of turning out differently than predicted. Turnout in one precinct might be higher than expected and voting machines might malfunction. Bad weather—a flood, for instance—might make it difficult for citizens to get to their precincts and cast their ballots.

Yancey always concluded his detailed election plans with a quote from Dwight D. Eisenhower as he plotted the Allied invasion of Europe during World War II.

*Plans are nothing,* Eisenhower said. *Planning is everything.*

Yancey repeated Eisenhower's dictum every election cycle. Here's our plan, he said. This has everything plotted to the inch, to the minute, to the hour. It's a good plan, but it probably won't mean anything once the voting booths are closed.[2]

## EVERYTHING IS PREPARATION

**B**e prepared. No journalist in the country went to work on September 11, 2001, thinking about how to cover terrorist attacks on New York City or the Pentagon. None of the student reporters or editors at *The Collegiate Times,* the student newspaper at Virginia Tech, had a plan to cover a homicidal assault on students and faculty in April 2007. No one at the Charleston, South Carolina, *Post and Courier* anticipated the sofa store fire that killed nine firefighters later that same year.

Every journalist learns the importance of preparation from hard and sometimes painful experiences. What you learn today may seem trivial, but it may be the very thing you desperately need when confronted with the unimaginable and the unexpected. Just as you should prepare an emergency kit before disaster strikes, you need to build up your own journalistic reserve:

▪ Study what other journalists have done in crisis situations. Read their stories, watch their videos and listen to their audio reports. While no stories should be duplicated, learn what has worked in other situations. Don't hesitate to adapt a good idea to your circumstances. This isn't a call for plagiarism; rather it's taking what worked for someone else and making it your own.

▪ Make a formal checklist of the key sources—official and unofficial, both on and off your beat—you'll need to get in touch with in an emergency. Keep it available some place portable, such as on your phone. Stay in touch with old sources and develop new ones; someone you just got to know could be the person you need to turn to in a crisis. Save business cards and collect phone numbers and contact information on your computer and phone. Keep a hard copy too, because technology is not foolproof. Hard drives crash and cell phones get stolen, so make backups!

▪ Pay attention to your colleagues' sources and the information they uncover. Clip or download those stories so they're available for quick reference.

▪ Keep detailed notes from interviews. Something you recently learned on your beat may be the key that later helps you understand a complicated issue. Be a packrat when it comes to picking up documents or information sheets you find at public forums or private settings. Develop a filing system that is organized, fast and works for you.

▪ Get out of your office and beyond your comfort zone. A visit to an unfamiliar neighborhood may give you the mental map to find a street you'll need to get to fast someday.

▪ Don't forget the mistakes you've made in the past. The memory of an error in your last story will keep you from making the same one when you're covering a crisis.

## CHANGING YOUR PLANS, AND FAST

 uring the Roanoke flood, reporters immediately headed out to the scene. Their mission was daunting but simple, and it can serve as an example for you if you have to cover a crisis.

1. **Get out there and find out what's going on.** Talk to as many people as you can about what has happened to them, their families and their homes. Get as close to the story as you can and pull together the details that will help your readers and viewers understand the magnitude of what has happened.

**2. Be enterprising, but don't be stupid.** Don't risk your life to cross a flooded street (as a couple of reporters in the Roanoke flood did), but do your best to get to the places where the flooding is the worst. Use common sense when you're in a situation that could quickly turn dangerous.

**3. Be professional, but remember that your needs as a journalist should not be your only concern.** Don't forget your humanity. You are a journalist and also a citizen, and you have a responsibility to the community. Saving people, setting up shelters and organizing relief operations were the priorities in the Roanoke flood. Those priorities may apply in your crisis as well. The TV news helicopter didn't hesitate to rescue the people on top of the grocery store. Dr. Nancy Snyderman, NBC News' chief medical editor, performed triage, sewed patients up and cleaned dirty wounds when she covered the devastating 2010 earthquake in Haiti.

**4. Stay in touch with your editors.** Check in regularly while you're out on the scene. You need to know where the action is, and the newsroom may have more up-to-the-minute information than you do. You also want to make sure you're not working on a story that a colleague is chasing. Use text-messages or Twitter to let your newsroom know what you've found out and to get updates and directions. Communication is an essential part of any coverage plan.

## CONCLUSION

The numbers documenting the flood's damage and destruction were staggering: Ten people died in the Roanoke Valley, eight by drowning. Another dozen were killed across the state.

Damages to Roanoke's businesses and infrastructure were estimated at nearly $83 million in 1985 dollars. Across Virginia, damages were estimated at more than $750 million.

The toll was higher in neighboring West Virginia. Nearly 50 West Virginians died and 9,000 homes were damaged. Twenty-nine of the state's 55 counties were declared disaster areas, and the damage estimate totaled $600 million.

Most of your days as a journalist will begin with a plan, and some days you may even follow through with it. But many things will not go according to expectations. Often, you will find yourself in situations for which no plan could have been imagined.

Sometimes, the stories that surprise you will have happy endings. Cherish those occasions. You may never have to cover a flood, tornado or war. With luck you will never have to write about a terrorist attack or talk to students who have survived an assault by a deranged gunman. But you must understand that at some point you will be asked to write about something you previously thought was unimaginable.

When this happens you must think through your options and contingency plans clearly and calmly. Marshal all your education, training and experience to assess the situation and act appropriately. As a journalist, you must be able to make as much sense as possible of the unthinkable, and you must then be able to present a fair and rational account to your readers and your viewers.

Be prepared. Your public is counting on you to do your part and so are your colleagues. Don't let them down.

## checklist

- **Know your community.** The previous chapter discussed the importance of understanding your community. Learn where to go and who to talk to *before* the unexpected happens. Develop sources *before* the crisis strikes; it may be too late afterward.

- **Stay calm even when the world around you is going crazy.** A newsroom covering a crisis can be a madhouse, with lots of people giving directions, some of them contradictory. Remember what the flight attendants say before the plane takes off: In the event of an emergency put your own oxygen mask on before you help anyone else. Apply your own figurative oxygen mask by taking a deep breath and collecting your wits.

- **Think through how you will deal with the people you come in contact with.** Your assignment is to get the story, but you have a responsibility to treat everyone you meet with dignity and respect. Too many stories are told of journalists who were insensitive and manipulative of people who survived disasters or suffered trauma. Good journalists aren't rude. Remember that the people you write about are always worthy of your respect.

- **Take care of yourself.** It may not hit you until after your deadline, but you may become emotional about the people you meet and their stories. If you have a heart you will feel others' pain as you report their stories honestly and compassionately. Adrenaline will carry you only so far; at some point you need to stop and rest.

▪ **Be disciplined and practice, practice, practice.** You may be abundantly talented, but talent will do you little good if you haven't exercised and honed your skills. Practice always beats talent when talent doesn't practice.

## assignments

1. People who live where natural disasters frequently strike are advised to assemble an emergency preparedness kit that includes first aid supplies, non-perishable food, water and sturdy shoes. Draw up a list of the items for your own disaster kit that will help you cover a story in an emergency. Ask yourself:

    a. What kind of clothes and shoes should you pack?

    b. What reporting supplies will you need? Reporter's notebooks, for sure, but how many and what kinds of pens or pencils should you have?

    c. What about extra batteries for your digital recorder or your video camera?

    d. Will you need maps of your community?

    e. How will you access your contacts and how will you get in touch with them?

    f. What else should go into your disaster kit?

2. Once you've made your list, get your kit together. Have it ready in an easily accessible place such as your desk or your car. Make sure you can grab it and go if and when the time comes.

## notes

1. *The Roanoke Times* began its coverage of the 1985 flood with its afternoon edition on November 4, 1985, and continued reporting on the aftermath through the rest of the year. The special section, "Fury of a Flood," was published November 11, 1985, and is the source for much of the historical information included in this chapter.

2. Interview with Dwayne Yancey, June 11, 2008.

## CHAPTER 11

Speak up for those who cannot speak for themselves; for the rights of all who are destitute.

PROVERBS 31:8

# shine a light

Madeline Adams Tate was one of Roanoke's invisible people. She lived in a ramshackle house just a few blocks from City Hall and walked to day jobs as a housecleaner. She lived with a man named George Williams; they paid $50 a month for a house with no electricity and a wood stove as their only source of heat. When they went to sleep one cold January night, Tate lay down beside the stove to keep warm.

Sometime during the night the fire went out. Outside, the temperature dropped to eleven below zero, making it the coldest night in Roanoke since 1912. The next morning, Williams' relatives called police when no one answered the door at the house. Inside, police found Williams suffering from frostbite. Tate was on the floor beside the stove, wearing a dress, two blouses, a sweater, a bathrobe and boots. She had frozen to death. She was 76 years old.

Tate was buried four days later in a pauper's cemetery. Reporter Douglas Pardue described the service:

A few minutes was all it took. . . .

The funeral home people lowered the pine casket into the ground, got back in the hearse and drove away.

Wayne Harris started his faded red International tractor and, as gently as the tractor could, packed dirt into the grave. After he built a small mound, Harris turned off the motor, got down on his knees and placed a few flowers on the pile of dirt.

He also dug a hole for a small concrete marker.

No name was on the marker, just the number 978 for the 978th person buried in Coyner Springs Cemetery, the cemetery Roanoke provides for the poor. . . .

No. 978 had a name: Madeline Adams Tate.[1]

A spokesperson for the company that owned the house where Tate died regretted her death, but said their housing contracts required renters to provide their own heat. The city said it tried to help people who didn't have heat, but it hadn't been alerted in time to save Tate. In the end, the city picked up the $255 tab for her funeral.

Tate's death provoked *The Roanoke Times* to begin a years-long campaign of reporting about housing conditions for the city's poor. Pardue documented the number of substandard houses in the city—some 1,200—and interviewed the owners of the houses and the people who lived in them. The residents told him about the lack of heat and adequate plumbing that endangered the lives of children and adults who were already living on the edge.

Most citizens of Roanoke had considered Tate's story an anomaly, but Pardue's investigation opened their eyes. Few ever visited the inner-city neighborhoods just blocks from downtown, where many of the community's poorest and most desperate citizens lived. They rarely saw the rotting houses, infested with rats and lacking hot water and electricity. They certainly never saw or heard the stories of the people who lived in those houses or worked in those neighborhoods. Their problems were invisible to most of society.

tuds Terkel called people like Tate the *et cetera* of history—people who were left out—and spent much of his career listening to them and telling their stories. These days, though, news organizations find themselves with reduced staffs and resources. Many no longer consider it an essential part of their mission to give voice to the voiceless and to speak for the disenfranchised.

After Hurricane Katrina devastated the Gulf Coast in 2005, Pulitzer-Prize winning author David K. Shipler took news organizations to task for failing to cover poverty unless they were prompted by a major catastrophe or a new government program.

The surprise most Americans felt at seeing the poverty in New Orleans after Katrina hit was an indictment of reporters and editors around the country, Shipler wrote in *Columbia Journalism Review*.

"In an open society, nobody who had been watching television or reading newspapers should have been surprised by what Katrina 'revealed,' to use the word so widely uttered in the aftermath," Shipler wrote. "The fissures of race and class should be 'revealed' every day by America's free press. Why aren't they?"[2]

Journalists fall into the trap of covering only what government *does,* not what it *doesn't* do, Shipler said. When government neglects a problem, as it neglected conditions in New Orleans, the problem receives little attention until disaster strikes. If reporters spent a week at job training centers, legal aid offices and housing agencies, Shipler said, they would find more powerful stories than they could write in a month, "not about the programs themselves . . . but about the problems the programs aim to solve."

No problem, Shipler said, is solved unless light shines on it for all to see.

*The Washington Post's* Anne Hull talked about this light when Maine's Colby College gave her the 2008 Elijah Parish Lovejoy Award for her reporting about people living on the margins in America. Hull, who won a 2008 Pulitzer Prize for coverage of how veterans were neglected at Walter Reed Army Medical Center, said she aspired to be a journalist who was able to "shine a light into the eyes of someone who wishes to look away" to reveal the life of the poor and the powerless. She wanted to write "about the little guy who's on the receiving end," not the powerful and the rich.

"There are two kinds of journalism," Hull said. "There's journalism that is very important and holds the government accountable and holds powerful institutions accountable for what they're doing. But there's the other side of it, and that is writing about the little guy who is on the receiving end of this vise and is being neglected and forgotten. That's the kind of journalism that I tend to do, and that's the telescope I look through when I'm out reporting stories."[3]

Hull was inspired by James Agee, a journalist who chronicled the lives of Southern sharecroppers during the Great Depression. Agee's kind of reporting is still done, Hull said, but less frequently. In its place, she sees bloggers and Tweeters, working from a coffee shop and never visiting places without electricity or running water. Cutbacks in the nation's newsrooms have made coverage of the fringes of society rarer and rarer, she said.

"One of the casualties in the smaller newsrooms is covering poor people in this country," Hull said. "And our coverage of class has dropped off the radar."

## GOING BEYOND CONVENTION

You've learned about the importance of diversity in the stories you write and produce. To be diverse in your coverage means you must strive to represent and reflect your community in all its variety; its different races and ethnicities, political viewpoints, faiths, ideologies, social and economic classes, both genders and all sexual orientations. The notion is simple, but its execution complex. Many news organizations don't do a very good job of it.

As part of your commitment to journalistic diversity, you are responsible for giving a voice to the poor, the disenfranchised and other under-represented citizens of your community. It's your job to talk to people whose lives are often ignored by the media, tell their stories and make sure their issues are brought to light.

As a beginning journalist, you may find yourself too often relying on official sources and experts—the government officials, politicians, business and industry executives who exercise prestige and influence in the community. They are important, of course, but they reflect only a small slice of the citizenry. You miss opportunities to enrich your stories when you talk to the same sources repeatedly while neglecting citizens at the opposite end of the spectrum.

Broaden your notion of where to look for stories. As discussed in Chapter 8, it's easy to fall into the habit of going to the same places and talking to the same people. Don't ignore the fascinating and important things that happen elsewhere. Visit neighborhoods and communities you've never seen before, especially those that have been marginalized by much of society. If you go only to places that are comfortable and welcoming, you'll miss much of the real-world vibrancy of the civic life you seek to represent in your stories.

Step beyond the conventional notions of your beat to determine what's important. You may be responsible for covering government, business, police and courts, but don't depend solely on these institutions for all your stories. Look harder at how these institutions influence people's lives, and ask yourself questions from the perspective of those most affected by what's taking place:

- What will this action mean for the people of this community or neighborhood?
- Who will benefit?
- Who will be harmed?

» Are those without power or influence being heard, or are they being shut out of the process?

» For those who are shut out of the process, what can you do so their voices can be heard?

Tom Huang, an assistant managing editor at the *Dallas Morning News* and an ethics and diversity fellow at the Poynter Institute, believes journalists must initiate intelligent and informed conversations about what's going in society. In particular, Huang says, journalists must shine a light that helps citizens understand the aspects of their communities with which they are not cognizant.[4]

Huang believes citizens in a democracy cannot make good decisions about public policy matters until they understand how people will be affected by those choices. A person may have strong opinions about an issue—illegal or undocumented immigrants, for example—but those opinions may not always be grounded in facts. The journalist's job is to tell the story in human terms: Who are the real people involved in this story, and how do policy changes affect them? What are their lives really like? How are their lives different from and similar to the lives of other people in the community? What stake do they have in the community at large?

The stories you tell may not always be popular. Many people don't want to read or hear about folks who are different from them in terms of race, ethnicity, sexual orientation, physical ability or nationality. But Huang says you have a responsibility to continue presenting stories that show your community as it really is, not as some might wish it to be.

Your decisions in covering a story should be driven by journalistic values, not by a desire to be politically correct, to impress sources or to curry favor with business leaders. The business aspects of a news organization can be at odds with its journalistic purpose. View the people of your community as citizens first who may or may not be readers or viewers. Don't view them as customers who are defined by marketing demographics, attitudes and habits, to be divided into segments.

If you become too concerned with the market makeup of your audience, you can lose sight of the people whose stories aren't being told. Instead, you will concentrate on the segments of society attractive to advertisers—people with higher disposable incomes and political influence; those who live in the wealthiest neighborhoods and whose children go to the best schools. You may become fixated on telling your readers and viewers what they can do to improve their lives, how they can make themselves more comfortable, protect their investments and be entertained. There's nothing wrong with that as long as you don't forget the Madeline Tates and the other underserved members of your community.

Don't ignore those who are ignored by society at large. Look for the stories about people who are disenfranchised and lack resources and opportunities. Do not shirk your responsibility to speak for and act on behalf of those who have no access to traditional forms of power and influence.

## EXPLORING THE CULTURES IN YOUR COMMUNITY

As newsroom resources shrink, Huang worries that it will become harder and harder to devote reporters to communities that are not part of the mainstream. A reporter cannot begin to understand a different culture and its customs unless she spends days, weeks and sometimes months building relationships with people inside that community. If she isn't given adequate time by her news organization, she will never be able to write the stories that will make a difference.

One reporter who did receive the necessary time was Christina M. Woods when she was a reporter at *The Wichita Eagle*. Woods is African American, grew up in Wichita and went to Wichita State University, so she brought perspective and understanding to her cultural affairs beat. She didn't talk about *diversity* because the term caused some people to shut down when she approached them. Instead, she tried to cover Wichita's communities of color in a holistic way that recognized differences as well as commonalities. When she started her beat, she systematically met with people in the various communities to get to know them and to help them get to know her and *The Wichita Eagle*. Many had never been approached by a reporter before; they had no idea how to make their voices heard or get their interests covered. She asked for story ideas but also for suggestions about how the paper could improve its coverage. She visited with leaders in the Asian, Indochinese and Latino communities, gatekeepers who could explain what made their people unique and also introduce her to ordinary people who could further open her eyes to their cultures.

The stories of the gatekeepers are important, she says, but she always tried to keep her focus on ordinary people. She felt their stories illuminated issues and informed readers about what life is like for people who come from different backgrounds and have different perspectives.

Readers don't always appreciate a commitment to covering the richness of a community, as Woods learned from the response to a story she wrote about how blacks and Hispanics were coping with the recession. Some readers complained that she should not have singled out minorities because the economic downturn had affected everyone; a few even called her racist.

She defended her work in a Poynter Online column by stating that the groups she singled out typically experience higher levels of unemployment even in good economic times. She offered her critics the opportunity to talk about their experiences in future stories, but all declined.

"No one story can capture the entire scope of the economic toll on our readers, viewers and listeners," she said. "Tightly written, focused stories from various viewpoints can begin to broaden the coverage in telling ways. To me, such storytelling approaches aren't racist. They're inclusive."[5]

## A COMMITMENT TO COMPREHENSIVENESS

he Project for Excellence in Journalism has been a leading voice for journalistic responsibility for more than a decade. In one of its early statements, it made this important point:

> Yet, the surest way for journalism to survive is by emphasizing what makes it unique—its basic purpose and core standards. Even in a new era, journalism has one responsibility other forms of communication and entertainment do not: to provide citizens with the information they need to navigate the society. That does not preclude being entertaining or profitable—or publishing something merely because it's interesting. That does not mean journalism should not abandon failed habits in the way we present news.
>
> But it does imply a commitment to comprehensiveness, to offering certain information about democratic institutions, and to ordering information in some relationship to its significance so that people can use it as a map to travel through the culture.[6]

Comprehensiveness certainly includes stories about influential people, but it also means stories about people whose lives diverge from society's norms. As Anne Hull would say, your job is to shine a light into the eyes of people who want to look away. Do it with the understanding that many in your audience will not want to be reminded of the problems of people on the fringes of society. Your mission may not make you wildly popular with this sector of your audience, and you may also find yourself at odds with those who argue there's little business advantage to be gained from such reporting.

But if you don't do it, who will?

## UNDERSTAND THAT CHANGE CAN BE SLOW

Roanoke held hearings and conducted numerous poverty studies after Madeline Tate's death. In 1992 a task force issued a report of more than one hundred pages that said improving the educational system was key to fighting poverty. It listed 170 proposals, many of which could be implemented at little or no extra cost. It also called for a redirection of public and business spending and the creation of a massive local volunteers-against-poverty program to raise public awareness.

But the poor and their problems didn't go away. On January 20, 1996—almost eleven years to the day after Tate's death—a rental house in southeast Roanoke caught fire. Goldie Christine Duncan, a 46-year-old grandmother, died in the fire, along with her four grandchildren, ages three to six. An extension cord connected to an electric space heater caused the fire, which started on the first floor. The house had no smoke detectors, in violation of city code.

Reporters Mary Bishop and S. D. Harrington found that Roanoke's inner-city neighborhoods were still rotten, despite all the political pronouncements, task force studies and recommendations over the previous decade. Thousands of impoverished people still lived in decaying houses. The paper ran a series over three weeks detailing once more the problems and suggesting solutions to the situation.[7]

As before, city leaders were shocked. The mayor proposed a historic preservation fund and a construction investment fund for inner city neighborhoods. In his State of the City address, he urged the formation of a task force to investigate the inner-city's problems and to determine how much money should go into the funds.

The series reported that the city had looked into the problems of poor neighborhoods before—seven times, to be precise—over the previous 30 years. Each time the recommendations had been the same: Save and restore the old houses and the old neighborhoods or the whole city would suffer. Each time, the recommendations were ignored.

The slow pace of change and improvement could have been cause for despair for those on the front line in that war against poverty. It could also be disheartening for those who were writing and editing the stories about the living conditions of the poor. They might think, *Why weren't more people paying attention? Why didn't government act more forcefully? Why didn't more churches and civic organizations rise up in outrage?*

You will learn as you progress as a journalist that change doesn't always come as fast as you would like. That doesn't mean you should throw up your hands and walk away from important stories that need to be told and retold. *The Roanoke Times* continued its reporting on the lives of the city's poor and disadvantaged into the new century. Its coverage sparked public conversation and debate, and it led to improvements—some marginal, some significant—in the lives of some of the city's poor. But poverty wasn't eliminated in Roanoke, or anywhere else for that matter. Many poor people in this country continue to live in conditions that resemble those of Third-World countries. Too many children go to school undernourished and under-nurtured. Teen pregnancy rates remain distressingly high. Too many jobs pay wages too low to support a family. Public health programs allow too many people to fall through the cracks.

Don't despair. Martin Luther King Jr. said that the arc of the moral universe is long, but it bends toward justice. A similar faith keeps the best journalists plugging along, even when it seems only a few people are listening and paying attention.

The disadvantaged still need to be heard. Journalists will always have a job to do telling their stories.

## CONCLUSION

In one of Roanoke's old neighborhoods, a stone slab reads:

"The city forgot her. Madeline A. Tate froze to death 1/21/85."

People like Madeline Tate live in the communities you cover. Few people know about the desperate lives they lead, the poverty they endure, the shameful conditions that make up their daily existence. Telling their stories won't be quick or easy, but it is something you must do, with compassion and understanding.

It's your job to force society to pay attention, before the wood stove goes out on a freezing night, before the home burns to the ground, before the hurricane strikes.

Bring their stories into the light.

## checklist

- **Be aware of who you're writing about.** Review your sources and the stories you've written over the past month. Who are the people you talked to? How much variety and diversity is represented in your stories?

- **Review the places you've visited in the past month.** Where have you been? How many new places have you visited? Are you guilty of going to the same places for your stories? How much variety and diversity is reflected in your activities?

- **Make a list of new people to talk to and places to visit.** Be deliberate and methodical. Come up with a plan that will allow you to make new contacts on a regular basis.

- **Use multimedia to help you see diversity.** The rise of multimedia storytelling should heighten your awareness of the need for diverse sources for your stories. Videos and slideshows give you the opportunity to show a multitude of faces and to hear a range of people speaking in their own voices. If all your multimedia faces and voices look and sound the same, you will have failed to present an accurate picture of your community. Words have power, but pictures frequently have more.

## assignment

David K. Shipler said that if reporters spent time at job-training centers, food pantries, homeless shelters and other agencies that serve the poor, they could find powerful stories about people living on the edges of society and the issues that are important to them. When was the last time you visited one of these agencies and talked to the people they serve? Go to one and find a story—not about a social service program but about the problem the program is designed to address. Find the people who are affected and tell their stories.

## notes

1. Interview with Douglas Pardue, March 24, 2009. His story about Madeline Tate's burial ran January 26, 1985, in *The Roanoke Times*.

2. David K. Shipler, "Monkey See, Monkey Do: If Pols Ignore Poverty, the Press Does, Too," *Columbia Journalism Review,* November/ December 2005.

3. Anne Hull, 2008 Elijah Parish Lovejoy Convocation, Colby College, Waterville, Maine, September 28, 2008. Available online. www.colby.edu/news_events/c/b/092808/1537895/2008-elijah-parish-lovejoy-convocation-anne-hull/. Accessed April 12, 2011.

4. Interview with Tom Huang, December 30, 2008.

5. Interview with Christina Woods, January 9, 2009.

6. www.journalismtraining.org/action/provider_detail?id=757.

7. Interview with Mary Bishop, August 31, 2008. "The Invisible Inner City," a series by Bishop and S.D. Harrington that explored poverty in Roanoke, ran June 1–21, 1997.

## CHAPTER 12

A well-instructed people
alone can be permanently
a free people.

JAMES MADISON

# be a watchdog

A new reporter at the *Belleville News-Democrat* was cleaning her desk when she came across an Illinois state manual and asked veteran reporter George Pawlaczyk if he wanted it. Pawlaczyk flipped through the document called "A Report to the Governor and the Inspector General" and saw a story about a child who had died while in the care of the state's Department of Children and Family Services. Pawlaczyk was amazed: the report cited similar cases but did not contain the names of victims, caseworkers or references to when or where the children died, but it detailed specific errors that had been made by state workers who were supposed to be protecting the children. By reading the details, Pawlaczyk and Beth Hundsdorfer, another *News-Democrat* veteran, recognized a local case in which a baby died when her mentally ill mother delivered her into a waste-filled toilet. They figured there had to be a way to find out who the other children were and to link them to the mistakes that had contributed to their deaths.

Pawlaczyk and Hundsdorfer began to match the small details with state records called *child death summaries,* which contained information about when and where children had died, again without names. The reporters used these anonymous accounts to find out what had happened to other children who died due to

DCFS errors and negligence. For four months they talked to coroners, police and sheriff's departments across Illinois to track down official records that helped them build a database to verify the names of the dead children and details about what had happened to them.

They discovered that over a seven-year period, 53 children in Illinois had died under the care of child welfare workers who were supposed to protect them. Welfare workers who made fatal mistakes were sometimes disciplined, but rarely were they suspended or fired. Other times records were altered after a child's death to shift blame.

The details were horrific:

    A six-year-old girl was punched in the stomach by her mother's boy-friend and left to die in the snow on Christmas Day. A DCFS investigator failed to check with police about a previous episode involving the boyfriend that could have alerted her that the child was in danger.

    A four-month-old girl was beaten to death after a caseworker let her stay with her crack-addicted mother. The caseworker had allowed the mother to continue smoking the drug as long as she agreed to drop the child off at a neighbor's house first.

    A nine-year-old girl suffering from cerebral palsy starved to death even though caseworkers had visited her home 33 times.

The stories of deaths and neglect went on and on. In all the cases, the state agency had either ignored or failed to properly investigate earlier reports of child abuse or endangerment.

Readers around the state were sickened by the revelations, and so were Illinois legislators. Lawmakers enacted new regulations to make the child welfare system more accountable.

Thanks to the commitment and dedication of a feisty news organization and its hard-nosed reporters, real changes were made that would likely save children's lives.[1]

ome of your work as a journalist will be hard-hitting, but some of it will be on the lighter side as well. There's nothing wrong with entertaining your readers or viewers while informing them, just as long as you don't lose sight of your most important mission. At its core, your primary duty is to serve as a watchdog, looking out for the interests of the public that you serve. Many people assume that watchdog responsibilities fall only to veteran investigative reporters, but all journalists should see themselves in this light, no matter what their beat may be. If you take your mission to heart, you'll find there's nothing more satisfying, honorable or important than serving as a watchdog.

Good journalists hold society accountable at all levels and give ordinary citizens the information they need to make sound decisions to lead safe and healthy lives. As watchdogs, they look hard at government, education, businesses and utilities, non-profits, the criminal justice system and the health care industry. At their best they even cover their own organizations critically and aggressively. They uncover secrets, find truth behind lies, clarify distortions, dispel rumors and expose corruption and unfair practices. They reveal dishonesty, incompetence and injustice. They ask questions about systems, programs and agendas, pointing out flaws that allow abuses to occur, and seek solutions when possible. They hold public and private powerbrokers accountable, and they listen to and give voice to people who have little or no influence.

Your watchdog work can take many forms. It can be a major investigation into institutional failures, such as Laura Frank's stories for *The Tennessean* and the now-defunct *Rocky Mountain News* about how the U. S. government stonewalled compensation claims by nuclear arms workers who became sick or died building atomic weapons.[2] You may uncover consumer hazards, such as the *Chicago Tribune*'s stories about the failure of federal agencies to protect children from hazardous toys, car seats and cribs, or the *Milwaukee Journal Sentinel*'s series about poisons in everyday materials, such as baby bottles and microwave-safe plastics. You may question how public officials use and abuse their power, as in the *Detroit Free Press'* series about corruption in the mayor's office or Pulitzer Prize-winning stories by the *East Valley Tribune* of Mesa, Arizona, about a county sheriff's campaign against illegal immigrants.

Large newspapers, including *The New York Times* and *The Washington Post,* are known for their watchdog attitude, a tactic often called *accountability journalism.* That same zeal can be found in smaller dailies, such as *The Belleville News-Democrat* and the *Post and Courier* in Charleston, South Carolina, and in weeklies such as the *Willamette Week* in Portland, Oregon, and *The Mountain Eagle* in Whitesburg, Kentucky. Even though newspapers have traditionally devoted more resources to watchdog work than other news media organizations, some television stations, including WFAA in Dallas and KHOU in Houston, and the television news shows *60 Minutes* on CBS and *Frontline* on PBS, have strong watchdog reputations. Non-traditional news organizations have assumed a watchdog responsibility as well. ProPublica is an independent non-profit newsroom that's committed to investigative journalism on a national scale; it offers its stories to traditional news organizations to publish or broadcast, and it also posts its stories on its website. Other news organizations have gone online to get their stories out to the public. VoiceofSanDiego.org, The St. Louis Beacon and MinnPost.com are nonprofit online operations dedicated to local watchdog work.

Watchdog journalism can often take months to produce, but it can also be turned around in a day or two. It sometimes requires significant time and money, resources that are in short supply in many news organizations today. What it needs most to thrive, though, is dedicated journalists who are committed to producing stories that tell what is really going on and give people the information they need to change systems, institutions, policies and, occasionally, leaders.

Someone like you.

## FREEDOM OF THE PRESS, AND THE RESPONSIBILITY THAT COMES WITH IT

**A** watchdog mindset is a key component of your civic obligation as a journalist. The First Amendment allows you to go about your work without government interference or restraint. With this privilege comes responsibility. You must never lose sight of how freedom of the press is tied to the other freedoms enumerated in the First Amendment. Citizens have the freedom to speak and the right to gather peacefully and to petition their government when they think change is needed. For people to exercise their freedoms wisely, however, they must be fully informed about what government and other institutions are doing. Journalists must monitor those centers of power and tell the people what's going on so they can make decisions and take action.

"Information is now a public service as much as it is a commodity," Scott Lewis, an executive editor of VoiceofSanDiego.org, told *The New York Times.* "It should be thought of the same way as education, health care. It's one of the things you need to operate a civil society, and the market isn't doing it very well."[3]

It's your responsibility to fill that gap. Look at the world critically and skeptically and alert people to the changes that affect their lives. Doing this well requires you to go beyond what Bill Kovach in *Nieman Reports* calls a "simple journalism of witness." Kovach urges reporters to probe beneath a story's surface, challenging assumptions and assertions to generate reporting that "invites a civic judgment."[4]

Pulitzer Prize-winner Maurice Possley says the best watchdog journalism sheds light on things that otherwise would not be seen. It shows people the great difference between how things are supposed to work and what is really happening.

Watchdog journalists know their stories will make some people uncomfortable and angry, particularly those in power. That's all right. An old definition of journalism says it should comfort the afflicted and afflict the comfortable. That's still a good rule of thumb for the craft. Don't be afraid to shake things up.

## ADOPTING AN ATTITUDE OF WATCHDOG JOURNALISM

The *Belleville News-Democrat* has fewer than 50 people on its news staff, but the paper has always been high performing, city editor Gary Dotson says. It faces competition from the much larger *St. Louis Post-Dispatch,* a paper with a proud heritage. Long ago, though, *The Belleville News-Democrat* decided that it would out-hustle the *St. Louis Post-Dispatch* as the local watchdog.

Since then, the paper's track record of watchdog journalism has grown long and impressive. In the 1990s it broke stories about sexual misconduct by local Roman Catholic priests long before such abuse became a national scandal. In 1992 the newspaper revealed that Belleville police racially profiled black motorists to keep African Americans out of the city. To prove their case, reporters and editors compiled a database analyzing 175,000 citations issued by Belleville cops. The results prompted the U. S. Justice Department to look into the matter, and the city entered a consent decree to stop the profiling. The paper uncovered property scams by landlords in nearby East St. Louis, and in 2002 it revealed how housing inspectors and armed police officers illegally entered homes to check for occupancy violations. In 2005, Pawlaczyk pulled a trash bag from a garbage bin outside a state employment office. Inside the bag he found more than 100 records that had not been shredded as required by the state. The records listed clients' names, addresses, birth dates, home telephone numbers and Social Security numbers—personal information that identity thieves could use to obtain credit cards to commit financial fraud.

Pawlaczyk and Hundsdorfer's series about the failures of the child welfare system in Illinois won a 2007 Robert F. Kennedy Journalism Award. In 2009 the team began an investigation into the harsh conditions inside a supermax prison that was intended to house the most violent Illinois inmates. They discovered that one-fifth of the prison's inmates—many of them suffering from mental illness—had been held in solitary confinement for up to 10 years. They continued their investigations as public watchdog groups and state and federal officials pressed for reforms. The prison series won the prestigious George Polk Award.

Dotson, who also serves as the paper's projects editor, says *The Belleville News-Democrat* is committed to watchdog reporting, but with a difference from many news organizations: Every reporter is expected to contribute to the effort. He describes his newsroom's culture as one in which the DNA of watchdog reporting is ingrained in every beat reporter. Instead of a single investigative reporter or team, watchdog reporting is fostered throughout the newsroom. The result, Dotson says, is that watchdog journalism at the paper is an "attitude rather than a project."[5]

Watchdog stories can come from anywhere. Often they come from tips or hunches, but rarely from an editor's ideas, Dotson says. A good watchdog reporter keeps her ear to the ground, questions things that don't seem right, and then checks them out.

*The Belleville News-Democrat* reporters approach small stories as well as large ones with a watchdog mindset. If a new fire chief is hired, the beat reporter is expected to check his background, to find out where he worked before, what he did and what he didn't do. Reporters routinely file Freedom of Information Act requests for payroll and travel records and check criminal histories of elected and appointed public officials.

Read documents carefully, Hundsdorfer says.

"Highlight, make notes in the margins, go where they send you. For example, if a police report mentions an order of protection, go get it. If an order of protection leads you to a divorce file, get it," she says. "Think of it as a treasure hunt for information."

"Question authority," Pawlaczyk says. "Don't take a government official's word at face value. Use common sense. These are the qualities that can lead to big stories that can lead to changes and help the downtrodden, and can right even the most egregious of wrongs. Investigative reporting is not rocket science."

*The Belleville New-Democrat*'s approach doesn't always sit well with people in power. The paper has been sued numerous times, and a county board chairman once ordered employees not to talk to Pawlaczyk. The paper's reporters and editors are proud of the recognition they've won for their work. Their commitment to watchdog journalism has paid off in important ways at a time when most news organizations face declining readership or audience numbers. For a decade beginning in the late 1990s, it was the only newspaper in Illinois or Missouri to see its circulation grow each year.

## The investigative reporter's top 5 tools according to Gary Dotson

1. **FOIA requests.** Good stories are often buried in public documents. If you have a hunch about a story, but a government official or resource officer is standing in the way, submit a Freedom of Information Act request.

2. **Court documents.** If it's in a court file, it's a public record and you are entitled to view it, regardless of whether the case is pending or closed. They include depositions, subpoenas, motions for discovery, orders of protection and search warrants.

3. **Public records.** These include city budgets, government audits, police reports, pension records, state annual reports and property records, to name a few. If it involves tax dollars, it should be a public record, and many are available online.

4. **Form 990s.** Tax-exempt charities and non-profit organizations must submit these to provide annual financial information to the Internal Revenue Service. They are public records.

5. **Shoe leather.** Develop good sources, go door-to-door, talk to people in bars or grocery stores. Ask them what they know and how they know it. People are a valuable resource for information.

## MANAGING YOUR RESPONSIBILITIES

**W**atchdog journalism isn't easy, and it's not always exciting. In fact, it can be mind-bogglingly dull to pound the pavement, gather documents and talk to sources while simultaneously juggling your daily reporting duties.

After the *Rocky Mountain News* closed in 2009, Laura Frank helped found the Rocky Mountain Investigative News Network. She's now the executive director of I-News, which delivers multimedia reports to news outlets across the Rocky Mountain region. In a 2008 workshop she conducted for investigative reporters and editors at the University of Illinois, she offered tips for how reporters can manage their watchdog responsibilities while working their daily beats. Among her suggestions:

- **Keep a list of ideas gleaned from your daily reporting.** She cites a technique recommended by editors at the Lexington, Kentucky, *Herald-Leader* called the two-notebook theory. Keep one notebook for daily work and a second for enterprise stories, which are projects that aren't tied to events or assignments but grow out of tips and information that you gather on your own. Use your free time to ask questions and do research for stories in your second notebook.

- **Sell a prospective story to your editors by giving them a minimum and maximum plan.** Outline for them what you think you can provide at the very least and at the most. Even at the least, you'll still have a story you might not have gotten otherwise.

- **Be organized in your reporting.** Figure out who the major sources are for your story. Frank says it's usually best to start on the periphery with general sources and work your way to the center as you build up your knowledge. Be sure to look for sources who might disagree with your premise and talk to them. Always look for documents and data that can add substance to your story.

- **Be organized in your interviewing.** Keep detailed notes and files for different topics.

- **Make to-do lists daily of what you've done and what you need to do next.**

- **Write as you report.** Frank believes this will help you see the holes in your story and alert you to the need to change directions. Don't freak out if you do; that's why you do the reporting.

- **Fact-check everything.**

- **Ask for feedback from your sources.** They may give you follow-up ideas.

### HOW WATCHDOGS CAN SAVE NEWS

**W**atchdog journalism is at risk in many newsrooms today because of budget and staff cuts. Because in-depth reporting can take time and may not even result in stories, some newsrooms have decided to use their limited resources to produce stories that are reliable but routine—the "simple journalism of witness" that Kovach decries. As experienced reporters retire, many newsrooms find themselves with gaps in leadership and knowledge that could take years to fill.

Current trends could be counterproductive. Many journalists believe that watchdog journalism and investigative reporting are keys to the survival of their newsrooms.

Tim McGuire, the former editor of the *Minneapolis Star Tribune,* has argued that newspapers in particular must maintain their watchdog role if they are to remain relevant. "Few things can be as important to a community as strong, penetrating investigative work," he said in a speech to journalists at Washington and Lee University in Lexington, Virginia. "Journalists who highlight problems, challenges, opportunities and successes of communities can revitalize newspapers. Investigative reporting is in the public interest, and it can win readers like few other things you can do."[6]

David Boardman, executive editor of *The Seattle Times*, says news organizations cannot afford to abandon watchdog reporting.

"In an age when our critics love to crow that news is an undifferentiated commodity available everywhere, investigative reporting clearly isn't," he wrote in an issue of *Nieman Reports* devoted to watchdog journalism. "It's something that newspapers do that hardly anyone else can afford to: spending weeks, months and sometimes even years uncovering important stories that powerful people and institutions don't want the public to know."[7]

Boardman describes how the watchdog tradition at his paper evolved with beat writers teaming with investigative reporters to uncover medical abuses, art fraud and athletic scandals at both the high school and college levels. All the stories caught the public's attention, sold papers and drove Web traffic, and led to changes in institutions and programs.

In 2006 the *Milwaukee Journal Sentinel* created a watchdog team that grew to 10 people and includes a major Web presence called Watchdog Online. The paper has tried to extend the watchdog approach to the work of its daily beat reporters and also created a beat called Public Investigator that focused on quick-hit consumer-focused watchdog stories. The beat's motto: "Taking tips, chasing leads, solving problems."

Its efforts have paid off. The paper won a 2008 Pulitzer Prize for local reporting for exposing illegal pension deals that cost taxpayers $50 million. It also won the 2010 Pulitzer for local reporting for uncovering fraud and abuse in a child-care program for low-wage working families that cheated taxpayers and put children at risk. The stories led to a state and federal crackdown on providers.

Assistant managing editor Mark Katches wrote in the watchdog issue of *Nieman Reports* that readers pay attention to the *Milwaukee Journal Sentinel*'s watchdog efforts. The Public Investigator pieces are among the paper's most popular online stories, and other watchdog stories drive Web traffic as well.

A readership survey commissioned by the *Times Union* of Albany, New York, showed that 68 percent of the readers believe it is important for news organizations to investigate issues in the community. Readers said up-to-date news was the most important service the paper provided, but watchdog reporting was next on their list. Editor Rex Smith wrote that his paper's commitment to watchdog journalism is one of the things that will keep it vital even in tough economic times.

Readers do pay attention to the work of watchdogs:

> "Congratulations to the *Chicago Tribune*—the reporters, columnists and its editorial board," read a letter to the editor as the corruption scandal surrounding former Illinois Governor Rod Blagojevich began to heat up. "You have done a very good job of staying on top of everything political going on in Chicago, Cook County and the state of Illinois—especially corruption and trying to weed it out.
>
> "Our country . . . became the greatest country in the world partly because of its free press. If only other countries had this same freedom, the world would be a better place in which to live.
>
> "You have held your head high."[8]

A watchdog journalist can hear no sweeter words.

## CONCLUSION

Muckraker I. F. Stone was once introduced at a student journalism conference as an investigative reporter. Stone dismissed the term, saying it was redundant. All reporters should be investigative, he said.

That's the attitude at *The Belleville News-Democrat,* and it should be your attitude as well. Approach every story with a watchdog mindset and look for the untold story or the one that someone wants to hide. Not all of them will become watchdog stories, but more will than you might first imagine. You must be curious, skeptical, and always asking questions. Remember, your job is to tell people what is really going on and why, to get to the bottom of the story. Your mission is to alert ordinary citizens about the outrages and the injustices that the powerful want to keep secret.

You may wonder if you'll even be capable of doing this kind of work. When you start your professional career you'll have lots of responsibilities, and your editors will be on top of you for stories they must have for the next news cycle. Deadlines will be tight. You may worry that your news organization is small and doesn't have what it needs to pursue good watchdog journalism.

Get over it. Reporters and editors complain that they need more time and resources even in good economic times, and small news organizations have always been faced with limited resources. Yet the best journalists somehow always find ways to do the important work, on stories big and small.

Watchdog journalists realize this kind of reporting feeds their souls and makes a difference in the lives of the people around them. It's hard work, but it's also a lot of fun.

They also understand that if they don't do it, there's a good chance that no one else will, either.

A news organization's size does not matter; good watchdog reporting starts with journalists filled with zeal to tell people what's really going on. Big organizations may have more reporters on staff, but they don't have exclusive rights to watchdog journalism.

Make the watchdog attitude part of your DNA. You don't have to be a big dog to be a watchdog.

## checklist

- **Always ask how and why.** Follow I. F. Stone's advice to search beyond wrongdoers to find flaws in the system that allow injustices to occur. Look for ways that things can be improved.

- **Make it worthwhile.** Don't go after something that is not important. Your readers and viewers expect you to keep things in perspective, not to focus on the trivial or to be guilty of sensationalism.

- **Don't forget people.** Stories don't matter unless they're about real people. Show how people are affected by the problems or issues you're reporting on.

- **Be fair.** Your job is to follow the facts. Be curious and remain skeptical. Abandon preconceived notions when beginning a story.

- **Be compassionate.** Zeal is important, but it can also get you in trouble. Watchdog journalists need brains to do the work well and accurately and compassion to be fair.

- **Be comfortable with gray.** Sometimes you will uncover villains and scoundrels, but more often you'll find shades of gray. Accept the gray areas and resist painting people and organizations as strictly black or white.

▪ **Don't preach or be a scold.** Make your story as strong as it can be, but let your readers and viewers decide for themselves what you've proved. You don't need to tell them what to think.

▪ **Join Investigative Reporters and Editors.** You'll get ideas, advice and tips as well as access to thousands of stories in the IRE archives and a network of working journalists who can give you suggestions. *The IRE Journal* comes with membership and details how reporters at small and large news organizations do their watchdog work.

## assignments

1. The 2010 Pulitzer Prize for Public Service went to the Bristol, Virginia *Herald-Courier* for Daniel Gilbert's series about the mismanagement of natural-gas royalties owed to thousands of landowners in southwest Virginia. The award is vivid testimony that small news organizations and young journalists can produce top-notch watchdog journalism. The *Herald-Courier* has only seven reporters and a circulation of 33,000. Gilbert had been out of college for just four years and juggled his investigation with daily responsibilities. (He likes to point out that he covered an Easter egg hunt nine days before the Pulitzer announcement.) Read Gilbert's series at http://www.pulitzer.org/works/2010-Public-Service. Then read the *Nieman Reports* interview with him at http://www.niemanwatchdog.org/index.cfm?fuseaction=showcase.view&showcaseid=00127. Then answer the following questions:

   a. What lessons do you take away from his experience at a small paper?

   b. How can you put his example into practice in your own work?

   c. Brainstorm watchdog stories you haven't gotten around to investigating yet. Make a plan for getting started.

2. Laura Frank advocates keeping two notebooks, one for everyday reporting and one for investigative reporting. Start your second notebook; take note of the things you see and hear every day that raise questions about how systems work and don't work.

## notes

1. George Pawlaczyk and Beth Hundsdorfer, "Lethal Lapses," *Belleville News-Democrat,* November 19–21, 2006. Available online. http://www.bnd.com/236/. Accessed April 7, 2011; George Pawlaczyk and Beth Hundsdorfer, "Trapped in Tamms," *Belleville News-Democrat,* October 22, 2010. Available online. http://www.bnd.com/600. Accessed April 7, 2011.

2. Interview with Laura Frank, January 12, 2009; "Deadly Denial," *Rocky Mountain News,* July 20-23, 2008. Available online. http://www.rockymountainnews.com/staff/laura-frank/stories/. Accessed April 7, 2011.

3. "Web Sites That Dig for News Rise as Community Watchdogs," by Richard Perez-Pena, *The New York Times,* November 18, 2008.

4. Bill Kovach, "The Daily Work of the Media," *Nieman Reports,* summer 1998.

5. Interview with Gary Dotson, February 12, 2009 and November 9, 2010.

6. Tim McGuire, "Apocalypse Now! Reinventing Newspapers in the Public Interest," speech given at Washington and Lee University on May 3, 2005. Available online. http://journalism.wlu.edu/Reynolds/mcguire.html. Accessed April 7, 2011.

7. Rex Smith, "Remembering the Value of Investigative Journalism"; Mark Katches, "Investing in Watchdog Reporting"; David Boardman, "Making Firm a Newspaper's Focus on Investigative Reporting"; *Nieman Reports,* fall 2008, special issue on investigative reporting.

8. "Voice of the People," *Chicago Tribune,* December 13, 2008.

Always do right.
This will gratify some people
and astonish the rest.

MARK TWAIN

# do the right thing

ontroversy erupted on the University of Illinois campus when the February 9, 2006, edition of *The Daily Illini,* the independent student newspaper, hit the newsstand. It featured six editorial cartoons depicting the prophet Muhammad. In one of the cartoons, the prophet's turban was a lighted bomb. In another, the prophet clutched a knife, and in another devil's horns protruded from his turban. The cartoons had first been published in Denmark, triggering protests from Muslims who believed the images were sacrilegious. Their initial publication sparked riots and deaths in Nigeria, Afghanistan, Libya, Pakistan, Somalia and Lebanon.

Newspaper editors around the world debated whether to reprint the cartoons. Most newspapers in the United States chose not to publish them, while many European newspapers did, for a variety of different reasons.

Acton Gorton, the editor-in-chief of *The Daily Illini,* wrote an opinion piece that ran beside the cartoons in which he described the cartoons as "bigoted and insensitive," but criticized U. S. newspapers for not publishing them. How, he wondered, could he champion free speech and not present the cartoons for the public to see? Gorton said his decision had been gut-wrenching, but he hoped publishing the cartoons would create a "dialogue on the campus and in the community." He urged readers to express their opinions.

"Exercise your First Amendment right and don't be afraid to say something unpopular," he concluded. "As citizens, we have a right to use that freedom."[1]

Muslim students on campus quickly protested. One letter writer accused Gorton of committing "journalistic arson. . . . Just because Mr. Gorton has the right to reprint the cartoons doesn't mean he should reprint the cartoons. The profession of journalism carries a great responsibility. I feel Mr. Gorton has betrayed that responsibility."

Some applauded the decision. One letter writer said *The Daily Illini* editors showed "tremendous courage to defend freedom of the press in the face of possible destruction by Islamic religious fanatic terrorists." Another writer commended the paper for "its courageous stand in defense of freedom of speech."[2]

Members of the university community were not the only ones surprised by the publication of the cartoons. In an editorial the next day, the paper's other editors wrote that Gorton and opinion page editor Chuck Prochaska ran the cartoons without consulting the student editorial board, the publisher or the paper's paid editorial adviser. The editors said that while they did not necessarily disagree with the publication of the cartoons, they objected to how the decision was made and how the cartoons were presented to readers. Readers, they said, were talking about whether the paper was right or wrong to publish the cartoons instead of talking about what the cartoons represented to Muslims and non-Muslims.

Gorton and Prochaska responded in a column of their own, accusing the other editorial board members of a lack of courage and commitment to a free press and the First Amendment. Gorton and Prochaska said anyone who had been in *The Daily Illini* newsroom the night before publication knew the cartoons were going to be published. No one objected, they said, until the backlash started. Furthermore, the two editors insisted that Gorton, as editor-in-chief, had final authority over the paper's content.

"Free speech is all about more speech," Gorton and Prochaska concluded. "We will not resign. We will not issue an apology."

As a journalist you have learned how to gather information and put it together in a story accurately and fairly. You know how important it is to ask good questions and to listen carefully to the answers you're given, then to verify what you've been told. You understand the importance of seeing and hearing things with your own eyes and ears, and the need to understand the people and the places you write about. Each day you should grow more confident in your skills and abilities.

Yet, being a good journalist is more than simply gathering, writing and presenting the news. You must also learn how to make sound decisions about what you choose to report and what you choose not to report. Every story and picture you publish may impact the people in the community that you serve.

The decision-making process isn't simple. As you go about your daily work, you will be routinely challenged by stories and situations that will require you to make ethical choices about what to do and what not to do. There are no Ten Commandments, Hippocratic oaths, or step-by-step lists for journalists that you can memorize and consult for every circumstance you face.

Unfortunately, many citizens think that journalism ethics is an oxymoron. They've seen or heard about situations where journalists acted unethically. Some journalists have plagiarized material or made stuff up. Others have lied or misrepresented themselves to get information or pictures for their stories. And some have been rude or abusive toward people who have been thrust into the middle of stories through no fault of their own.

Yet journalism ethics is not a contradictory notion, and the vast majority of journalists do follow basic rules about how they do their jobs. The best ones understand the need to think critically about how they ought to do their work and how their work will affect the public and the subjects of their stories.

## ETHICAL CONSIDERATIONS

**A**cting ethically as a journalist requires you to think deeply and deliberately about what you ought to do or not do. It requires you to choose among the good and the bad options that you will face. Then it requires you to explain—not rationalize—what you did and why.

The ethical and moral issues you will face will come in many guises, and it won't matter the size of your news organization or whether you write for print, broadcast or online. What will matter are:

- The methods you'll use to gather information for your story.
- The consideration you give to the feelings of the people you write about.
- Information that is appropriate to include in your story and information that should be left out.
- Whether certain details enlighten and inform your readers, or merely sensationalize the story and needlessly offend your audience.

▪ Whether you go ahead with an assignment if you have strong religious or political convictions about the story you're assigned to cover.

The ethical considerations may also be blurred by legal concerns. Will your story damage someone's reputation? If it does, can you verify that your story is accurate? Even if it's verifiably true, is it something the public needs to know, or is it so personal and private that there's no compelling reason to disclose it?

These situations are complicated because you are not solely a journalist. You're an individual with family and social ties and special interests; you may identify strongly with a particular religious, ethnic or racial group. The combination of these attributes makes you a unique person, and they also influence your decision-making.

Sometimes you will have to cover stories you don't like or don't agree with. If you're the only reporter around when a sensitive story develops, you have a responsibility to cover it fairly no matter how uncomfortable or unpleasant it may be. While you don't always have control over the stories you're assigned, you can choose how you cover and present the story. If you have a sound process for making those decisions, you can avoid many of the pitfalls that journalists new and experienced alike confront in their daily work.

Chapter 10 talked about preparing yourself for the unexpected stories that will come your way as a journalist. Preparing yourself for ethical issues you are likely to face is just as important. No one can anticipate everything, but the more you think about the ethical dos and don'ts of journalism, the more you'll be able to make sound and justifiable decisions when confronted with a story that challenges your sense of right and wrong.

### Making ethical decisions

Even though no universal journalism code of conduct exists, most news organizations have professional standards that provide guidance on how you should go about your work. Many journalists follow the code of ethics for the Society of Professional Journalists. The code covers four broad areas that can guide you in your decision-making. Here's a summary:

▪ **Seek truth and report it.** Be honest, fair and courageous in the way you report and present information. Verify what you learn and seek multiple sources for all your stories. Don't mislead or plagiarize, and avoid stereotypes. Be aware of your own biases and work to keep them out of your stories. Distinguish between news reporting and advocacy journalism.

■ **Minimize harm.** Always treat your sources, the subjects of your stories and your colleagues with respect. Be compassionate toward people who may be adversely affected by news coverage and sensitive when dealing with children and sources or subjects who have no experience with journalists. Understand that your stories may cause harm or discomfort, and do your best to limit the harm while remaining faithful to the facts. Show good taste. Don't pander to lurid or morbid curiosity.

■ **Act independently.** Your first obligation should always be to the public. Avoid real or perceived conflicts of interest. Be aware of associations or activities that might damage your and your news organization's integrity and credibility.

■ **Be accountable.** You have a duty to explain to your audience and your colleagues how you go about your work and how you make decisions. Admit mistakes and correct them quickly. Hold yourself to high journalistic standards, and expose any unethical journalistic practices that you see.[3]

Keep in mind that this is a voluntary code, and no one can force you to follow it or any of the other ethical principles discussed in this chapter. However, not following this code can hurt your credibility and career. Adherence to these basic concepts helps you serve your public thoroughly, honestly and with integrity. That should be your goal in every story you undertake.

## Asking yourself good questions

Not only is it important to ask good questions to the people you talk to, it is also important to ask yourself good questions in order to make good decisions as a journalist.

When Bob Steele was director of the ethics program at the Poynter Institute, he compiled a list of questions to help journalists make ethical choices when faced with tough situations. They reflect many of the key points found in the Society of Professional Journalists Code of Ethics, and they can provide a strong basis for your own self-analysis about your methods, motives and the possible effects of your work. When faced with a situation in which you are unsure of what to do, Steele says you should ask yourself:

- What do you know, and what do you need to know?
- What is your journalistic purpose?
- What organizational policies or professional guidelines should you consider?
- How can you bring people with different perspectives and ideas into your decision-making?
- Who will be affected by your decisions?
- How would you feel if roles were reversed and you were the subject of the story?
- What are the potential consequences of your actions?
- Are there ways to minimize harm while remaining true to the facts of the story?
- Can you justify your actions to your public, the subjects of your story and your colleagues?[4]

Using these questions as a guide allows you to determine if the purpose behind your story is journalistically sound. If it is, decide how to fill in any information gaps that exist. Make sure you've talked to people on all sides of the story so you present diverse viewpoints fairly. If you see your story potentially causing harm, think about the legitimate ways to minimize such harm while staying honest to the facts.

Be open to questions and observations others might have, too. You may be confident in your news judgment, but always be aware that you have blind spots and biases, just like anyone else. Listen respectfully to the ideas and suggestions of other reporters and editors, which come from personal experiences unlike yours. You'll hear new ideas and insights; the more brains involved, the more likely you are to make a decision that you can justify to your audience, colleagues and yourself.

Welcome feedback from readers or viewers about the choices you've made. An honest dialog with your audience can open your eyes to the blind spots that you and others in your organization may be unaware of.

After you've consulted the professional codes, asked yourself the right questions and sought advice and guidance from others, you can be more assured of your reporting choices. You'll be able to explain your actions to yourself and others, confident that you've made thoughtful and proper decisions.

## Taking the time to do it right

Slow and deliberate are virtues even in the news business, where speed seems to take priority. You might admire the person who always seems to make the right call quickly, like a quarterback who can change a play at the line of scrimmage and throw a miraculous touchdown pass, but a hasty decision can be a bad one. The pace of online news cycles demands you get your stories posted before your competitors, but this can result in devastating errors. Haste led to premature reports of the deaths of U. S. Reps. Stephanie Tubbs Jones and Gabrielle Giffords. Haste led some to report NBC News host Tim Russert's death before even his family had been informed. Shirley Sherrod lost her job with the U. S. Agriculture Department in part because news organizations were in a hurry and didn't thoroughly check out a video that seemed to paint her as a racist.

You always want to be first with the story, but it's better to be second and right than first and wrong.

What to ask yourself as you go about your work:

- Are you fulfilling your journalistic duty to your readers and the public?
- Are you serving the public's interests or yours alone?
- Are you jeopardizing your credibility or the credibility of your news organization?
- Are you doing something that will make your readers not trust you or your organization?

## UNDERSTANDING YOUR FIRST AMENDMENT PRIVILEGES—AND RESPONSIBILITIES

Gorton and Prochaska were suspended from *The Daily Illini* for their decision to run the cartoons, and a student task force was created to investigate how the decision to publish was made and communicated internally. An unsigned editorial acknowledged that Gorton had final say on content as editor-in-chief, but emphasized that he also had a responsibility to consult others before making a decision of such importance.

The story captured national attention. *The New York Times* quoted Gorton saying he regretted not discussing his actions more fully with his staff and that he wished the paper had given the cartoons more context and explanation. But he had no regrets over publishing them and stood by his decision.

"My first obligation is to the readers," he said. "This is news."

A similar scenario played out differently at another university. The independent student newspaper at Northern Illinois University in DeKalb ran all 12 Danish cartoons on February 13, 2006. Where two editors made the call at *The Daily Illini,* Derek Wright, the editor in chief of *The Northern Star,* expanded his editorial board from 5 to 12 members to discuss the issue.

The editors voted 11–1 to run the cartoons. In a front-page editorial, editors called the cartoons tasteless, inappropriate and offensive. Nevertheless, they said they felt a responsibility to show readers the images, but in a way that was respectful and enlightening. The cartoons ran on a news page and were packaged with a local reaction story and a column by the co-president of the Muslim Student Association.

Wright said reaction to *The Northern Star*'s package was more positive than negative. He said Muslim groups disagreed with the decision to publish the cartoons but appreciated how the paper handled the matter.

"We discussed whether we thought it was newsworthy enough or whether we were just screaming First Amendment, printing it just because we could," Wright told *The News-Gazette* in Champaign, Ill. "We don't want to cause controversy just to be controversial."[5]

A news organization has an obligation to publish stories and photos—even editorial cartoons—that illuminate what's happening in our world. That duty can't be set aside when the news is unpleasant. Both *The Daily Illini* and *The Northern Star* had the right to publish the Danish cartoons, no matter how offensive and inflammatory they were to Muslims and others. However, even with the most careful consideration and planning, the editors still could not forecast the outcome. Once published, the cartoons failed to create a campus dialog at the University of Illinois about the real issues or how different people reacted to them. Instead of light, *The Daily Illini* generated only heat.

Potter Stewart, the late U. S. Supreme Court Justice, could have taught the editors a lesson or two.

Stewart was an ideological conservative who handed down centrist decisions during his term on the court. He said the federal government could not ban abortions, but it did not have to pay for them.

He said prayer in schools was okay as long as it was not coerced. He opposed capital punishment but did not consider it unconstitutional. He is widely remembered for declaring that, even though he could not define pornography, he knew it when he saw it.

Stewart was a champion of the rights of citizens as enumerated in the First Amendment to the U. S. Constitution: The government cannot restrict freedom of religion, freedom of speech, freedom of the press, or the freedom of people to assemble and to petition their government. In one of the court's most important free-press rulings, he sided with the majority that allowed *The New York Times* and *The Washington Post* to publish articles based on secret Pentagon Papers about the origins of the Vietnam War. By a 6–3 vote, the court held that the U. S. government's effort to block the articles before they were published was unconstitutional.

Stewart understood that the wonderful privileges the Founding Fathers gave the press carried obligations with it as well. In an interview with *American Heritage Magazine* after his retirement, he discussed the Pentagon Papers ruling. He said it was hard to imagine any justification for prior restraint short of national security.

But, Stewart said, the constitutional freedoms that journalists enjoy do not absolve them of higher obligations to act responsibly and even, on occasion, to censor themselves.[6] Journalists, he said, should not confuse their *right to do something with doing the right thing*.

Understanding this concept is key to fulfilling the pact you have with the public to provide information, understanding and enlightenment: It is simply not enough to say that you have a right to do something. You must also try to do the right thing.

Some of the information you convey as a journalist may anger people, just as some of it will please and delight others. Causing discomfort and creating disagreement is the result of keeping people informed. You will generate complaints and criticism, angry letters, phone calls, e-mails and blog postings. That means your work is reaching the public, where it can make a difference.

Just because the First Amendment says you can, however, doesn't mean you should. Be thoughtful and deliberate in exercising your free press rights. A working knowledge of the First Amendment is essential. Good journalists understand their responsibility goes beyond constitutional protection. Take to heart the responsibility of keeping people informed so they can understand their world, govern themselves effectively, and make their lives and the lives of others better.

## CONCLUSION

**Y**ears later Gorton still believes he was justified in publishing the Danish cartoons, but he says the issue was always more than just the First Amendment. He believes it was a journalistic imperative for *The Daily Illini* to give people a way to make up their minds about the cartoons and talk about what they meant and represented.

"I thought there would be some sort of earnest discussion about this, especially inside the college community," he said. "It was really an opportunity that was wasted."

The First Amendment requires a free press, but it does not require anything more than that. It does not require you to be fair, responsible, truthful, effective or even accurate. Yet you must be all those things and more if you are to do your job properly. If you accept the guarantee of freedom that the Constitution provides, you must ply your craft ethically and fairly, honestly and thoughtfully. Ask yourself whether you are making the right decisions about the content you choose to publish or not publish, whether you are treating your sources fairly, and whether you have a bias going into the assignment. Take the time to make sure the story is done accurately and correctly.

The right thing does not mean the easy thing, or shying away from controversial stories. The right thing means that you will think deliberately about what you do, and that you will exercise standards and principles that will ensure you make the right choices for the right reasons.

Know what you have the right to do, but try to do the right thing as well.

### checklist

- **Ask yourself good questions.** Are you fulfilling your journalistic duty to the public? Have you considered the consequences of your actions? Have you brought people with different viewpoints into your deliberations?

- **Study the First Amendment.** Journalists too often get hung up on the press clause and lose sight of how all five of the Amendment's guaranteed rights are interconnected. A good book to start with is Anthony Lewis' *Freedom for the Thought that We Hate: A Biography of the First Amendment* (Basic Books, 2008).

Study journalism ethics. If your school offers a journalism ethics class, take it even if it's not required. If no such course is offered, begin an independent study. You can find numerous studies in journalism ethics in such books as *Doing Ethics in Journalism: A Handbook With Case Studies* by Jay Black, Bob Steele and Ralph Barney (Allyn & Bacon, 1998) and *Media Ethics: Issues & Cases* by Philip Patterson and Lee Wilkins (McGraw Hill).

Keep the ethical discussion going with your classmates, coworkers and colleagues. What sensitive issues have they faced in their work? How did they handle them, and what did they learn from the experience? What worked and what would they do differently?

## assignments

The Code of Ethics of the Society of Professional Journalists can be found at http://www.spj.org/ethicscode.asp. The code for the Online News Association can be found at http://asne.org/article_view/smid/ 370/articleid/315/reftab/132/t/online-news-association.aspx. The link to the code for the Radio and Television News Directors Association is: http://asne.org/article_view/smid/370/articleid/313/reftab/132/t/rtnda-code-of-ethics-and-professional-conduct.aspx.

1. Review each of the codes, making notes about the points you feel are most important.

2. Create your own personal code of journalistic ethics over the next week, emphasizing the steps you would take to adhere to each point in your version.

3. Use your code as a checklist for the next half-dozen stories you work on, and evaluate how closely you were able to follow it. What did you learn to do and not do? What missteps did you avoid, and what happened that you regret or wish you could do over?

## notes

1. Interview with Acton Gorton, September 9, 2010. His column about the cartoons ran on *The Daily Illini* Opinions page on February 9, 2006.

2. The letters quoted ran on *The Daily Illini* Opinions page on February 10, 2006.

3. Society of Professional Journalists, "SPJ Code of Ethics," 1996. Available online. www.spj.org/ethicscode.asp. Accessed April 12, 2011.

4. Bob Steele, "Ask These 10 Questions to Make Good Ethical Decisions," Poynter.org, August 13, 2002. http://www.poynter.org/column.asp?id=36&aid=4346. Accessed April 8, 2011.

5. "Daily Illini not only student paper to decide to run controversial cartoons," by Jodi Heckel, *The News-Gazette*, February 18, 2006.

6. Robert Bendiner, "The Law and Potter Stewart: An Interview with Justice Potter Stewart," *American Heritage Magazine*, December, 1983.

# 14

Do not do to others that which
would anger you if others did
it to you.

SOCRATES

# remember
# your humanity

R alph Jackson Lassiter Jr. was hauling a load of PVC pipes from his
home in Florida when his truck hit a guardrail on an interstate bridge
in Virginia and plunged into a ravine. The fuel tank ripped open and
the truck caught fire.

Gary McCleland and a couple of other motorists pulled over and scurried into
the ravine to help Lassiter. They called to him and he answered. "We thought, 'Hey,
we can get this guy,' " McCleland said. " 'Maybe he's just busted up.' "

But when they reached the truck they saw the driver was trapped. They
pushed a PVC pipe through the window on the passenger's side, trying to give
Lassiter something he could use to pull himself out. But they couldn't get to him.

As the flames swelled, McCleland heard Lassiter say, "God have mercy." Then
Lassiter said a prayer.

Reporter Kimberly O'Brien told the story of the rescue attempt and Lassiter's
death in the next day's print edition of The Roanoke Times. At the time of publication, police had tentatively identified the driver, but O'Brien didn't use his name
because his family had not been officially notified.

O'Brien described how McCleland and the other drivers tried to save Lassiter. She included Lassiter's final words and prayer as reported by McCleland, ending her story with this description:

> Later, as the ambulance prepared to drive off, one of the truck drivers—it wasn't clear which one—handed a state trooper a small, wooden cross to keep with the body. [The trooper] said he would do everything he could to make sure that the cross made its way to the man's family.
>
> "I wish he went instantly so he didn't have to go through that," McCleland said as he swung up into his own truck.
>
> "But he didn't die alone. He had someone with him."[1]

A few days later, the paper published a letter from Loretta Follis of Oak Ridge, Tennessee:

> Doesn't it bother anyone else to read the last words of an unknown man? Doesn't the reporter have any respect for his family? Did she have to put out the gory details of the accident? I understand it is a news story, but why couldn't she have reported the accident and left out the rest?
>
> That unknown man was my only brother. . . . He may have been a stranger to you, just passing through your town, but he was a loving, caring brother, son and uncle to his family. He didn't deserve the disrespect he got from your newspaper, nor did anyone else in my family.
>
> Thanks to the people who tried to help him and to the man who gave the cross to the officer for my brother.[2]

Follis and her sister, Lisa Shedrick of Gainesville, Georgia, had read an online version of O'Brien's story. Even though O'Brien did not use Lassiter's name, Follis and Shedrick complained that the story carried too many details about his death.

"We were 99 percent sure it was him, but we were hoping it wasn't," Shedrick said later in a phone conversation. "It was so shocking to read."[3]

'Brien, a veteran reporter, did not write her story in haste. She approached it carefully, and she conveyed the despair the would-be rescuers felt when they realized they could not save Lassiter, a man none of them had met. Most importantly, she wanted readers to know that Lassiter had not been alone at the moment of his death.

Yet the victim's family reacted negatively. Shedrick understood that a news story about her brother's death was warranted, but she wished the story had been presented differently.

"It should have been a simple story," she said. "I'd try to write things so people don't get hurt when they read something."

Readers and viewers are sometimes unhappy with the way a news story is handled. Their complaints might be emotional rather than factual, but they are usually legitimate. A story may have contained an embarrassing or harmful error or been framed in a way that readers felt was unfair or not appropriate to the facts. The reporter may have not talked to enough people or to the right people.

Sometimes, though, the complaint is not that something is wrong but simply that a story was done in the first place. The story may have been about the reader's family or someone she cared about. The reader might ask the reporter: *How would you feel if this story had been written about someone you know or love?* Or, *How would you feel if it were about your mother or father, brother or sister, son or daughter?* Or even, *How would you feel if it were about you?*

Those are hard questions to answer. Reporters assume an awesome responsibility when writing about people who, sometimes for reasons beyond their control, briefly enter the public eye. They deserve to be treated with respect and dignity, so understand that your stories can have repercussions far beyond anything you might intend or imagine. Never lose sight of the humanity of the people you write about, no matter what their circumstances. Never forget the common bonds that tie all of us together, and keep in mind that whatever has happened to the people in your stories could also happen to you or someone you know.

Ask yourself these questions about each of your stories:

- How would you want to be treated if the tables were turned?
- Would you object to the way the story was presented?
- Would you object to the details that were included?
- Would you wonder why some important facts had been left out?
- How would you feel?

## LEARNING EMPATHY

Etan Patz was six years old when he left his home in lower Manhattan one morning to catch a school bus. He begged his parents to let him walk to the bus stop by himself. It was only two blocks, he was a good kid, and he lived in a close-knit neighborhood; his parents said okay. A woman and a mail carrier saw him waiting to cross an intersection. After that no one saw him again.

Police appealed to the public for leads and set up a toll-free number that garnered calls from as far away as California. Neighbors and volunteers plastered the city with posters with Etan's picture. Local and national media gave the story nonstop coverage for a couple of weeks. His disappearance sparked the missing children's movement, and Etan became the first missing child to be pictured on a milk carton. May 25, the day he vanished, was designated National Missing Children's Day in 1983, four years after he left his home to catch the bus to school.

No one was ever charged with his kidnapping, though a convicted child sex abuser is a prime suspect. Police say charges against the man are unlikely because they have no evidence or a crime scene. Etan's body has never been found.

Anna Quindlen wrote about Etan's disappearance when she was a reporter for *The New York Times*. His story continued to haunt her, and she wrote about it again in a 2004 *Newsweek* column headlined "The Great Obligation." Her column reflected on journalistic responsibility and how so many reporters have disgraced the profession by lying, making stuff up and mistreating the people they write about.

"Reporters are often asked about their obligation to readers," Quindlen wrote, "but perhaps the most important obligation is the one we owe the subjects of our stories."[4] This obligation, she said, goes far beyond simply getting the facts right. It extends to bringing understanding and respect to the often heartbreaking news about their lives.

She cited Pulitzer Prize winner David Halberstam, who said he learned the lesson when he was a young reporter writing obituaries for *The Tennessean*. For most people it was the only time they got their name in print. The stories needed to be accurate, but they needed to be written with sensitivity and compassion as well.

"All this makes you wonder if journalism schools should teach not just accuracy, but empathy," Quindlen wrote.

### Practicing the Golden Rule

You may not normally associate empathy with your work as a journalist, especially when you are taught to be an objective observer. But the people you're writing about will read your story and compare it to their own reality. They may come up to you on the street or call you at work to talk about something you wrote. Sometimes they'll compliment you and you'll feel flattered; other times they'll question why you wrote something the way you did, or ask why you included a particular detail. Some may wonder about your approach and your motives. They may say your story made them mad, or caused them pain or distress. They may ask, "Why you would do something like that?" Be prepared to answer these difficult questions.

Perhaps, like many beginning journalists, you were attracted to the business because of an idealistic notion of journalism's capacity to reform and improve society. Journalism's capacity to cause pain may not have been as apparent. Each story you write can do harm as easily as it can do good. Every act of journalism has a moral and ethical dimension because of its effect on people. As discussed in Chapter 13, you need to think deliberately about what you do as a journalist and why you do it. You also need to think about how you would feel if the tables were turned, and the story was about you or someone you knew.

Treat others the way you want to be treated. That's the Golden Rule, and it pertains to the people you meet and write about day in and day out. Living the Golden Rule requires, quite simply, that you empathize with the people you write about. Recognizing the humanity of each individual will enable you to approach people and their stories with compassion and respect.

### The empathetic *ah ha* moment

Quindlen wondered if all journalists have a moment in their careers when humanity and the story merge indelibly. It may come when they're writing about people who have endured a crisis or a personal loss, sometimes of an almost unbearable magnitude. For her, it came in writing about Etan Patz. For Christina M. Woods, who covered cultural affairs at *The Wichita Eagle,* it came early in her career when she wrote about an illegal immigrant who had been injured on the job at a local company. Shortly after her story appeared, immigration agents investigated the worker and had him deported. "I was angry," she said. "I realized that these aren't just stories, they are people's lives."[5]

Pulitzer Prize winner Maurice Possley was a rookie reporter for Chicago's City News Bureau when he called the home of a teenager who had apparently jumped to his death from a Chicago hotel. Before Possley could ask a question, the boy's mother said her son had not come home from school yet. She didn't know he was dead. "I'll call back later," Possley told her.[6]

You don't learn empathy by reading or studying stories, Quindlen said. You get it by covering them, by imagining yourself in the place of the people you interview and write about.

Etan Patz was declared legally dead 22 years after he disappeared, but his story still captivates journalists. Etan's father still clips their stories, even though his original reason—to give them to his son when he finally returned home—is gone.

"I leave you with that image for those times when you think what you do is fleeting," Quindlen wrote to aspiring journalists. "The closest thing this man has to the body of his son is the body of your work. If that doesn't make you want to do better, find another job."

Photographer Alan Kim was taking his young sons to school on April 16, 2007, when an editor in *The Roanoke Times'* Blacksburg bureau called. Two Virginia Tech students had been shot to death in a dormitory, and the shooter was now rampaging through the engineering building. Kim rushed to the campus and became the first photojournalist to document the carnage. When the shooting stopped, 33 students and faculty, including the shooter, were dead. It was the worst mass shooting in U. S. history, and it thrust the Virginia Tech campus into the international spotlight.

Horror stories of media malfeasance soon emerged. Packs of reporters and photographers, many of them unwilling to take "no comment" for an answer besieged students. Tracy Schmidt, a young reporter for *Time,* heard a reporter from Kentucky hollering to a crowd of students: "I need a student from Kentucky. Anyone from Kentucky?"[7] Camera crews swarmed around a sobbing student on the drill field. They kept the cameras running when she asked them to leave her alone. One national journalist presented himself as a family member in order to get into a hospital room for an interview.

The staff at Virginia Tech's student-run *Collegiate Times* found themselves in a troubling situation; the victims were their friends and classmates. They tried to go about their job sensitively and professionally, helping to identify as many of the victims as possible. They mined Facebook and other social networks to track down the names of the killed and injured, and they tactfully approached friends and family members for confirmation. The student paper was the first news organization to confirm and post names of many of the victims.

*The Roanoke Times* managing editor Carole Tarrant directed her staff to cover the story in a way that informed readers while acknowledging the grief and hurt that pervaded the entire community. Get the news, she said, but do it with respect. The paper was determined to keep its focus on the people in the community.[8]

Greg Esposito, who covered Virginia Tech for the paper, lived in Blacksburg and was one of the first reporters on the scene after the shootings. He tried to remember that he and the other local reporters would still be around after the satellite trucks and national reporters left.[9]

*(continued)*

Donna Alvis-Banks, one of the lead reporters on the story for *The Roanoke Times*, had grown up in the area and knew it well. "You knew it was this big story," she said. "But you didn't want to do more harm. You needed to take care of your community."[10]

She learned what not to do from the way some reporters treated people in Blacksburg and on campus. By mid-week, she said, many students and residents simply refused to talk to any reporters, whether they were local or not. People posted signs that read, "Media go home. Leave us alone."

"The other media made it hard for us," Alvis-Banks said.

She tried to put herself in the place of the victims and their families. She didn't try to trick anyone; she told them up front who she was and that she wanted to have a conversation with them. If they wanted to be left alone, all they had to do was tell her.

Covering the story took an emotional toll on many reporters, but especially those with local ties. Alvis-Banks said she didn't sleep well for weeks after the shootings. Randy Jessee, an editor at the *Richmond Times-Dispatch* and a Virginia Tech alumnus, came to Blacksburg to help direct his paper's coverage. He said he wept every day that he was back on campus that April.[11] Amie Steele, editor-in-chief of *The Collegiate Times*, told her staff that anyone who couldn't bear the emotional strain could go home. About half left; those who stayed committed themselves to the story.[12]

Esposito said he and a colleague went to church the Sunday after the shootings, not for a story but to worship and pray. Someone asked if they were Virginia Tech students, and they said they were reporters. A church leader reacted suspiciously and told them everything they heard that day was off the record.

"It was like because we're journalists we can't be affected by this," Esposito said.

But Esposito and his colleagues were affected by the story, just as you will be affected by similar circumstances. Never apologize for it.

## CONCLUSION

Good journalists are not disconnected from the world they cover. Be fair, impartial and true to the facts of your stories, but don't remove yourself from the world around you.

People are at the core of every story you do; they are subjects worthy of your respect. Treat them the way you would want to be treated.

You will write about people like Ralph Lassiter, Etan Patz and the victims at Virginia Tech, and their stories will gnaw at you long after you've moved on to other things. You must remain true to the facts of your story, but treat the people you write about with empathy and minimize harm, even when it's hard or seems impossible, or when a deadline pulls you in another direction.

You're in a profession in which you tell people's stories. What an honor that is. Craft those stories honestly and fairly, but with compassion and—most importantly—with humanity.

## checklist

- **Treat people with respect and dignity.** You're catching people at their most vulnerable. Be thoughtful and considerate. If they've suffered the loss of a friend or family member, don't be afraid to express sorrow at the loss, but don't say you understand how they feel because you don't. Recognize that people have their limits, and learn when to back off.

- **Remember the humanity of the people you write about.** You can't ignore how a person died, but don't lose sight of how she lived her life. Encourage people to tell you the stories of the person's life. Try to find out what made her unique.

- **Be sensitive about what to include and what to leave out.** Details are important to your story, but learn the difference between pertinent details and the ones that are merely sensational or gory. Leave out nonessential details that could be offensive.

- **Remember the Golden Rule.** Ask yourself how you would feel if the story were about someone you cared about.

- **Get it right.** Accuracy is the foundation of what you do as a journalist. It's especially important when you're writing about a person who has died. Go back to your sources to double-check facts and details.

- **Know your own limits.** An emotional story will take its toll on you, too. Rest when you can. Don't be ashamed to talk about your feelings with a colleague or a supervisor. Seek professional counseling if you feel overwhelmed by your experiences.

## assignments

Stories about death and personal tragedies are among the most difficult for journalists, so learn how to approach them properly. Spend a week reading a local newspaper or news website and compile a file of the stories that deal with death or injuries.

1. Determine how the stories treat the people involved, particularly if they became part of the story through circumstances outside their control. Did the writer show compassion toward the subjects while striving to remain faithful to the facts of the story? Did you find some elements questionable or objectionable? If so, why do you think the writer included them? Were they essential or sensational? How would you have felt if the story were about you or someone you knew well?

2. Consult the Code of Ethics for the Society of Professional Journalists (www.spj.org/ethicscode.asp) and pay particular attention to the section on minimizing harm. Do the stories you collected comply with these guidelines? Detail in writing how the stories stand up to the SPJ standards.

## notes

1. Kimberly O'Brien, "Fiery Death Claims Trucker in I-81 Wreck," *The Roanoke Times,* May 11, 1999.

2. Loretta Follis, "Description of accident was offensive," *The Roanoke Times,* May 28, 1999.

3. Interview with Lisa Shedrick, June 1, 1999.

4. Anna Quindlen, "The Great Obligation," *Newsweek,* April 19, 2004.

5. Interview with Christina M. Woods, January 9, 2009.

6. Interview with Maurice Possley, January 24, 2009.

7. Interview with Tracy Schmidt, January 25, 2009.

8. Interview with Carole Tarrant, September 1, 2008.

9. Interview with Greg Esposito, August 4, 2008.

10. Interview with Donna Alvis-Banks, September 1, 2008.

11. Interview with Randy Jessee, August 2008.

12. Interview with Amie Steele, February 2, 2009.

I won't back down,
no I won't back down

TOM PETTY

# stand your ground

hen *The New York Times* reported a national study that showed casual sexual encounters—"hook-ups"—were a growing trend among high school seniors, student editors of *The Statesman* at Stevenson High School in Lincolnshire, Illinois, immediately recognized a local angle. They knew kids who bragged in the halls about the same kinds of things. *The Statesman* staff decided to take an in-depth look.

Jordan McNamara, the managing editor for content, and other editors knew the story would be controversial, but that didn't worry them. Barbara Thill, the newspaper's adviser, had been recruited from another high school a few years earlier with a mandate to create a paper that would be lively, engaging and represent the voice of the students. Under her guidance, *The Statesman* tackled provocative subjects such as teen suicide, oral sex and prescription drug dealing on campus, and as a result the paper had won state and national recognition for its work.

Stevenson students talked openly with the paper's reporters about how often they hooked up. They explained the term *lap tag* and said that "getting felt up isn't a base anymore." Some students seemed nonchalant about their sexual

153

activities, while others voiced regrets. One acknowledged that alcohol contributed to the frequency of hook-ups.

The student journalists tried to put the trend into context with a sidebar about a teenage couple from the school who were in a committed relationship. Reporters asked the school's teachers to describe their dating habits when they were in high school, and they interviewed a psychologist who said hook-ups could have lasting emotional consequences for both partners. A social worker warned students that it would be even harder to resist such encounters when they got to college. In another sidebar, which proved to be the most controversial, a junior provided a detailed timeline of how he hooked up one evening at a basement party.

Thill had trained her journalists to be aggressive and careful. McNamara and the other editors insisted that reporters get as many details as they could on the record and then verify the information they collected. Quotes from interviews were sent to sources to verify their accuracy. If the information wasn't right, McNamara said, corrections were made.[1]

The editors and Thill recognized the sensitive nature of the stories and showed them to the chair of the English department, who ran the journalism program. Even though most students who were quoted had agreed to let their names be used, the department chair suggested they be identified only by their first name and their graduation year. Another administrator approved the references to alcohol use in the stories, Thill said.

The Statesman distributed its 3,400 papers in bins around the school on Friday, January 30, 2009. On Monday all the bins were empty, which struck Thill and others as odd. Papers were almost always left over; their disappearance spawned a firestorm of controversy that engulfed The Statesman, its staff and Thill for the rest of the school year and beyond.

Administrators, some of whom came to Stevenson after Thill's arrival, said they had warned Thill and her editors about what they saw as problems with accuracy and balance; for them, the hook-up story crossed the line. A school spokesman told the Chicago Tribune the hook-up stories had little news value and recklessly exposed the identities of the students who were interviewed. He also complained that Statesman reporters did not seek comment from students who opposed hooking up and accused the paper of unethical behavior in printing the timeline story, saying it was a "how-to guide for sexual predators."

School officials said they couldn't trust Thill's judgment and stripped her of final authority over content in the paper. They bristled at allegations that they were censoring stories that put Stevenson in a bad light. An administration spokesman said the issue was shoddy journalism, not censorship.

Not everyone agreed. Parents supported Thill and her students at a school board meeting, and professional journalists rallied around The Statesman. The Chicago Tribune hinted in an editorial that school officials had confiscated some of the papers that disappeared so quickly. But school officials didn't back off. The administration crafted plans to restructure Stevenson's journalism program and

Thill's newspaper class. Instructors with no journalism background or experience as newspaper advisers would join the program.

Thill said she believed the administration had little tolerance for the hard-hitting stories that had become the hallmark of *The Statesman,* particularly ones that exposed problems at Stevenson. The hook-up edition, she said, simply gave school officials an opportunity to turn the paper into one that didn't upset people.

The more Thill learned about the administration's plans for the journalism program and the paper, the more she realized she couldn't work under the new restrictions. In early April, she called staffers together for an emotional meeting. Rather than submit to the new oversight rules and the new plans for the journalism program, she said she would step down.[2]

Thill could have kept her job and gone along with the new requirements, McNamara said.

"But she said, 'I can't work under those rules. That is not how I learned journalism and it is not what I teach and I will not practice what is opposite of what I practice and teach,' " McNamara said.

"She made a stand."

T hill is not the only journalist who has quit or been fired for refusing to compromise on a matter of principle. A journalism adviser at Naperville Central High School, also in Illinois, lost her job when she criticized her principal's response to the school paper's stories about drug use, which included a column containing profanity. Steve Smith, the editor of *The Spokesman-Review* in Spokane, Washington, quit rather that agree to job layoffs he believed would damage his paper's ability to cover the news. *Los Angeles Times* editor Dean Baquet and publisher Jeff Johnson were fired when they publicly defied corporate demands to cut the newsroom staff.

Just months after winning a Pulitzer Prize in 2008, Maurice Possley left the *Chicago Tribune* because he was convinced the paper's commitment to criminal justice journalism was flagging.[3] Ann Marie Lipinski, the *Chicago Tribune*'s editor, also resigned in 2008 because she disagreed with the direction that new management wanted the paper to take. Josh Prager, a senior writer in the *Wall Street Journal*'s New York City investigative unit, resigned because, as he wrote in a memo obtained by *Politico,* he believed that the future of long-form journalism was at risk under the regime of Rupert Murdoch, the *Wall Street Journal*'s new owner.

All of these journalists took a stand that cost them jobs they loved.

## WHAT DO YOU STAND FOR?

**A**s a beginning journalist, you probably have not spent a lot of time thinking about what you might do when forced to take a stand on principle. More likely you're focused on honing the skills you need to launch your career. However, at some point you may find yourself in a situation where you're asked to do something you simply cannot do in good conscience. You may be asked to go along with something that deep down you find objectionable or that crosses a line. It may not even require an action on your part; it may be a matter of simply acquiescing to the status quo.

There will always be assignments you would gladly hand over to someone else. You may cover stories about violence, tragedy and trauma that may haunt you for years, just as the story of Etan Patz haunts Anna Quindlen. You may question your own faith and beliefs when you write about poverty, illness and despair. It's natural to identify with the pain and anguish of the real people you write about (that's the humanity talked about in Chapter 14), and you may wonder if you can face another story of tragedy that results in unanswered questions. Journalists have a responsibility to report on sad and disturbing events that make up news. You can't ignore them. Everything you're learning now is part of your training for how you approach such stories. Talk about your misgivings with your editor and colleagues; they may have faced similar issues on other assignments, and they can help you find a way to handle the facts sensitively and professionally.

However, you must distinguish between the painful stories all journalists face and matters of conscience and principle. What will happen when you are confronted with a situation that requires you to take a stand that might ultimately cost you your beat, or even your job? Are you willing to take a stand as a matter of journalistic principle? Will you listen to your conscience, or will you be swayed by other considerations? Examine your position carefully, and answer these questions as honestly as you can:

- **What is your stand?** Don't be vague about matters of conscience and principle. What are the rights and wrongs involved? Enunciate what troubles you in as much detail as possible.

- **Why do you feel this way?** Are you being asked to violate your professional values? Are there personal values—religious, ethical, social, political—at stake? Again, detail these principles as clearly and completely as you can. Weigh your values and beliefs carefully.

▪ **What's the other side of the issue?** Your supervisors and editors have reasons for their positions. Talk to them about your misgivings and ask what they hope to accomplish. Listen to their answers with an open mind; their reasons may convince you. What compromises would alleviate your concerns? Is there a middle ground that would satisfy both you and your bosses? Most importantly, what will best serve the public interest?

▪ **What happens if, after weighing all options, you say no?** Will you simply be removed from the assignment, or will you face more serious consequences such as suspension or even firing? Are you willing to go that far?

The answers may not be easy, but maintaining your integrity as a journalist requires you to confront them.

## Personal and professional integrity

This text has examined how ethical guidelines provide a template for how journalists should conduct themselves. The rules deal with things you must do (get facts right, explain how you got your information, be fair and balanced) as well as things that are prohibited (making things up, presenting someone else's work as your own, misleading with words or images, sensationalizing or blowing things out of proportion).

Apart from these professional codes, you should set your own personal standards that determine not only what you will do but also what you will not do, even at the expense of a promotion or your job. No matter where your code takes you, your standards should start with a sense of personal and professional integrity. The Society of Professional Journalists code says professional integrity is the cornerstone of a journalist's credibility. The Radio–Television News Director's code says electronic journalists must report the news with integrity and independence. The code for the American Society of News Editors says journalism demands integrity as well as industry and knowledge.

The dictionary definition of integrity is basic but antiseptic: "firm adherence to a code, esp. of moral or artistic values; the quality or state of being complete or undivided." The word itself comes from the same Latin root as the word *integer,* which means a complete entity. Perhaps it's fitting that there is no commonly used adjective form of the word. It's not a description but a state. You have it or you don't.

Law professor, cultural critic and novelist Stephen L. Carter wrote about the virtue in his 1996 book *Integrity*. It requires three steps, Carter said:

1. Discerning what is right and what is wrong.
2. Acting on what you've discerned, even at personal cost.
3. Declaring openly that you are acting on your understanding of right from wrong.

He elaborates:

"The first criterion captures the idea of integrity as requiring a degree of moral reflectiveness. The second brings in the ideal of an integral person as steadfast, which includes the sense of keeping commitments. The third reminds us that a person of integrity is unashamed of doing the right thing."[4]

Carter says one reason integrity is such an important virtue is that it precedes nearly everything else. "The rest of what we think matters very little if we lack essential integrity, the courage of our convictions, the willingness to act and speak on what we know to be right," he explains.

## Develop moral reflectiveness

Always approach your work with a strong sense of its moral ramifications. This includes remembering that your stories are about real people. Your words and images can have positive or negative effects on people, and you must carefully weigh what those effects might be.

Moral ramifications go beyond stories. Reflect deeply on what really matters about your work as a whole. Develop a sense of what you stand for as a journalist so that you can approach your craft with an attitude of public service, understanding that your responsibility to citizens comes before business interests. Everything you do reflects on your colleagues, which reinforces the notion that you are responsible for acting honorably.

## Know where your values lie

Editors and other staffers at *The Statesman* came close to resigning en masse after Thill stepped down in the spring of 2009. McNamara said the students were frustrated with the restrictions that had been imposed on them. The school administration was disorganized and had no idea what it was doing with prior review, and the relationship worsened in the last months of the school year. Those final editions, McNamara acknowledged, were of dubious quality.

Thill insists that her decision to resign as *The Statesman* adviser should not be seen as heroic, but others disagree. In July 2009 she received a First Amendment award from the McCormick Freedom Museum in Chicago for her work as a high school newspaper adviser and for the principles she espoused. In her acceptance speech, she lamented the restrictions that many student journalists labor under.

While many students learn about the Bill of Rights in social studies classes, Thill said, they are not allowed to practice the First Amendment in their journalism classes. In fact, she said, students in many schools receive no information about their rights and responsibilities as citizens.

She told about John L. Young, a principal she worked for at another school who did understand the role of student journalists. When the student paper ran a story demonstrating how easy it was for an outsider to gain access to the school, Young commended the staffers. "You caught us with our pants down," he said.

Other administrators, she said, would have put the paper under prior review, as they did at Stevenson. Such administrators don't understand the job of student journalists.

"These administrators would never tell math students to miscalculate their figures," Thill said. "They would never tell the quarterback of the football team to intentionally throw an interception. They wouldn't ask a member of the choir to sing a false note. Yet in school after school . . . administrators will order or pressure student journalists to publish only happy news—fluff—only safe and comfortable stories that are often just an expanded school calendar."

She accepted the award on behalf of *Statesman* staffers who endured attacks, she said, "the likes of which no one, especially students, should have to endure."[5]

Quitting would have meant the administration won, McNamara said, and staffers couldn't abide that.

"We wanted to put [the paper] out for Ms. Thill and for ourselves so it wasn't [the administration] getting what they wanted," he said.

"They didn't win."

For all the turmoil, though, McNamara cherished his experiences at *The Statesman*, especially for what he learned about himself, Thill, other staffers and the school.

"You have to understand where you stand on these issues," he said, "because if you don't know how you feel or how you think about a certain subject you're going to be lost when you're confronted with this. . . . You have to know where your values lie."

The student editors who took over the paper after McNamara and other staffers graduated did their best to produce the kind of work that their predecessors and Thill had championed. At the beginning of the 2009–2010 school year, reporters and editors started working on a number of enterprise stories about controversial issues at Stevenson.

Administrators quickly objected.

In November Stevenson officials stopped *The Statesman* from publishing a story about drinking and smoking by honor students. In December they blocked a story about teen pregnancy and drug use, and they prohibited a story about prescription drugs and their side effects. The story quoted a student who took birth control pills to control her menstrual cycle. The girl gave the paper permission to use her name.

Senior Pam Selman, the editor-in-chief, told the school board on December 17 that the journalists felt bullied and intimidated.

"The fact that we are students does not deprive us of our rights as journalists working on a limited public forum to be free of unreasonable restraint," Selman said.

The administration didn't change its decisions. In January, five top editors and 11 of 14 staffers resigned in protest.

"I'd rather practice no journalism than journalism that doesn't follow with my ethics and what I believe in," Selman told the *Chicago Tribune*.[6]

### CONCLUSION

Thill and the student journalists at *The Statesman* followed the three steps Carter says are essential for acting with integrity. They determined that they were right in their efforts to report what was happening at Stevenson and that the administration was wrong in its attempts to block their stories. They acted courageously on what they discovered, realizing their stand could (and did) ultimately cost them their newspaper jobs. Finally, they stood their ground in explaining their actions and the principles that compelled those actions.

You have to know where your values lie, McNamara said. You must be willing to act on them, no matter the personal cost. That's what integrity is all about.

You alone must decide what you stand for and what you stand against as a journalist. No one else can do it for you. Have the courage of your convictions to speak and act on what you believe is right.

Don't sell out. That was one of the lessons Ben Gish learned from his parents at *The Mountain Eagle* in Whitesburg, Kentucky. All journalists must learn that lesson in order to do our work in an honorable way. As you strive to be the best journalist you can be, you may win honors and recognition, and you may find yourself in a well-paying job that has lots of influence. Don't let it go to your head. People will eventually forget the stories you write and the awards you win.

Integrity is all you have, in life and in your work. If you lose it, you may never regain it. Protect it in everything that you say and do.

## assignments

One simple definition of integrity is doing the right thing when no one is watching. But each of us must decide for ourselves how we define and embody this important concept.

1. What's your definition of integrity? What are the standards and principles that are most important to you, both as a journalist and individual? What do you believe in so deeply that compromise is impossible? Write down your definition and list your unbendable principles. Take your time and be thoughtful.

2. Using your list, evaluate the personal and journalistic decisions you've made over the past week. Are your actions in accord with your beliefs? Are there discrepancies? What practices or attitudes might you need to adjust?

## notes

1. Interview with Jordan McNamara, September 21, 2010.
2. Interview with Barbara Thill, May 1, 2009.
3. Interview with Maurice Possley, January 24, 2009.
4. Stephen L. Carter, *Integrity*, Basic Books, 1996, p. 7.
5. Thill provided the text of her remarks, which were delivered on July 25, 2009.
6. Dan Simmons and Lisa Black, "Stevenson paper's editors resign," *Chicago Tribune*, January 21, 2010.

## CHAPTER 16

> Whatever our personal frailties may be, the nobility of our calling will always be rooted in two commitments difficult to observe: refusal to lie about what we know, and resistance to oppression.
>
> ALBERT CAMUS

# commit journalism

Twenty-one police officers and detectives crowded into Barry Bearak's small room in Harare, the capital of Zimbabwe. Men with rifles guarded the door while others searched for clues to prove him guilty of a crime. They found two passports. One with his visa showed that he had entered the country as a tourist. The other contained papers that showed he was a reporter for *The New York Times*.

"You're a journalist?" they asked.

"Yes," Bearak said.

"You're not accredited in Zimbabwe?"

"No," Bearak admitted.

Bearak and Celia Dugger, his wife, became co-bureau chiefs of *The New York Times*'s Johannesburg bureau in early 2008, and Bearak went to Zimbabwe in March to cover the presidential election between incumbent Robert Mugabe and opposition leader Morgan Tsvangirai. Mugabe had ruled the country since its liberation from Great Britain in 1980; he was dictatorial, corrupt and cruel. The initial election results indicated that Tsvangirai had won, but the Mugabe regime refused to release official results.

No free press existed in Zimbabwe, and Bearak and other journalists had to protect themselves and their sources. As the stalemate lingered reporters became less cautious, identifying themselves and their affiliations at news conferences and asking tough questions. Bearak filed several updates daily for *The New York Times* website and dictated from his notes over a mobile phone as he worked in downtown Harare. On April 3, 2008, he went back to his lodge to file another story. Around four in the afternoon, he stepped out of his room for a break.

A female detective yelled at him, and several men quickly surrounded him. *Who are you?* they wanted to know.

A detective sneered that Bearak was guilty of gathering and disseminating news and that he would face charges of "committing journalism." The cops hauled Bearak and another reporter to the Harare Central Police Station where they were thrown into jail cells.[1]

o matter how small the town, people everywhere deserve thoughtful, impartial journalism, *The Roanoke Times* reporter Mary Bishop once told a college audience.[2]

In fact, Bishop said, they more than deserve it; they need it. A democracy requires it.

That's never been truer than it is today, and it may never have been harder than it is today, either. The past few years have been hard for journalism. Many newspapers have shut down, while others have slashed staffs, cut the space for news and drastically reduced international coverage. The audience for network and local television news continues to decline. Cable news shows have increased their ratings, but in the process they became ideologically polarized, producing a journalism of strident assertion rather than one of verification. More people have turned to the Web for news, but online operations have struggled to find an economic model that can sustain the cost of producing quality journalism. Alternative news sites have launched bold experiments, but many have been financed by philanthropies or wealthy individuals. Whether they can sustain themselves remains an open question.

Despite all these problems, you have decided to be a journalist.

Congratulations. The field needs people who aren't afraid of challenges and who understand journalism's importance to society. The journalism you produce over the next decades will be different in many ways from the journalism of previous years. Newspapers and broadcast news may survive in some fashion, but much of your work will be online; some of it will probably be produced and transmitted in ways that we can't yet imagine. Even though the methods of delivery and consumption will change, you must remain committed to the fundamental values and practices that have sustained good journalism for generations. As a member of the next generation, your duty is to provide the journalism people deserve and need.

Journalism is not a commodity like a box of tissues or a roll of paper towels, and the citizens who need it—readers, viewers and listeners—understand this. Journalism is a public good; its vitality and strength stir people. Tyrants and dictators outlaw it, and the corrupt try to foil it. It lives and breathes in the communities where it is practiced fairly and honorably.

People pay attention to good journalism. Sometimes they agree with it, and other times they argue over it. It can make them laugh and make them cry. It can anger and even outrage them. If you practice journalism well, you will reflect what's going on in the world in a comprehensive and proportional way, and you'll give citizens stories and information that will stir them to action. If you do it half-heartedly or frivolously, citizens will let you know. The bonds of trust and credibility that you establish with your audience are fragile. If you break them, you may not be able to restore them.

Journalism needs people like you who are committed to it as both a craft and a profession. This is not to discount the contribution of citizen journalists and amateur bloggers who keep tabs on what goes on in their neighborhoods and beyond. Citizens have always augmented the professionals. The more eyes and ears on the government and schools, the police, the courts system and the other institutions of society, the better; their additional independent observations only increase the flow of information and news.

As much as citizen journalists do, they have other occupations and interests, and they won't always sit through the four-hour meeting, monitor the trial or go to the scene of the accident or the blighted neighborhood to talk to landlords and their tenants. Communities will always need full-time journalists who will commit themselves to the hard digging, the hellacious hours, the worry and the second-guessing that are required to consistently produce stories that matter.

It needs people like you.

## GETTING PERSONAL

ou may have been wondering about the person who collected the stories for this text. I was a newspaperman for 32 years. For 29 of those years I was a reporter and editor at *The Roanoke Times* in Virginia, where I worked both with rookies who were still learning how to write basic stories and with experienced reporters and editors who taught me far more than I ever taught them. I was involved in big stories and small ones, from killer floods and blizzards to major investigations of public officials and public policies. Three of our projects were finalists for Pulitzer Prizes.

In 2004 I began teaching journalism at the University of Illinois at Urbana–Champaign. Leaving the newsroom was difficult. After spending a third of a century doing the same thing (although working in a newsroom day in and day out is never the same thing), making such a major change was scary.

As an editor, I considered myself a teacher first. I worked with people to help them do a better job of telling readers what they needed and wanted to know about the world around them.

Going into a classroom was a challenge, but I felt I had something to offer a younger generation of journalists. Lots of things have gone wrong with the practice of journalism over the years. If I could give beginning journalists a little guidance about how to do journalism properly, well, I thought that would be good use of my time.

When I left the newsroom, I still believed in journalism as a force for good in our society. I couldn't go off to teach journalism if I didn't believe in it.

I told my colleagues that, most of all, I believed in them, and trusted them to do the right thing by their readers, their co-workers, and their community.

Now, I put my faith in you and trust that you will act honorably. The news business will continue to change in ways that we may not be able to imagine. Throughout it all, remain true to the values and principles that have made journalism a force for good in society. Build on the work of your predecessors and protect the profession against those who would debase it.

Never forget that the purpose of journalism is to serve the public, to give citizens the information they need to be free and self-governing. Keep the people in the forefront of all that you do. They depend on you to give them information to help them navigate the world around them. Do not look upon them as objects, customers, market shares or focus groups. Never lose sight of their humanity. Their stories are at the heart of what you do. Telling their stories is a privilege.

## ONE LAST CHECKLIST

he work you'll do as a journalist is important to the people you write about, to the people you write for, and for our democratic society. It's impossible to put everything you need to know as a journalist in one text; you'll be learning for your entire career. But some key points to keep in mind in order to commit excellent journalism are:

- **Be accountable to your public.** They should know how you gathered the information for your stories, who your sources were, the methods you used, what holes still exist. Be as transparent as possible.

- **Be accountable to your colleagues.** They depend upon you to do your job professionally and honorably. Your journalistic missteps will reflect poorly on them, just as theirs will reflect poorly on you. Lean on each other for advice, solace and feedback. Give them support when they need it, and welcome their help when it's your turn.

- **Be accountable to yourself.** Protect your integrity and your credibility; if you lose them, you may never regain them. Resist pressures to compromise the core principles and standards that all of us hold dear.

- **Don't worry about fame.** Telling the truth will not make you popular. Be satisfied with doing your job well and occasionally hearing a word of thanks from a reader or viewer. That ultimately means more than any prize or award.

- **Keep things in perspective.** We are bombarded with news and information 24/7; the result sometimes seems like non-stop hype. Not everything demands instantaneous attention and comment, so take a deep breath and try to see things they way they really are. Your readers and viewers need you to help them put events in context, not to frighten or worry them needlessly.

- **Embrace new technology, but don't let it rule you.** New tools are wonderful, but they are a means to an end, not the end itself. They may help you find sources and information, but they can't replace the need to talk to people in person, hear what they say, and comprehend and explain their happiness, sadness, pain and anger. The world is complicated; it cannot be reduced to 140 characters or less.

- **Aspire to do great things with your journalism.** Even if most of your stories are small, incremental—even ephemeral—you can still reach for the peak of Mt. Everest with your other stories. Find stories that right wrongs, solve problems and correct injustices. Act as a watchdog on the powerful and influential, and give voice to those who are ignored by society.

- **Don't wait for inspiration.** Work hard instead.

- **Be humble.** You don't have all the answers; you don't even know all the questions.

- **Remember how important every story is to someone's life.** Be thoughtful about what you write and whom you might carelessly and needlessly injure. Make sure what you're doing is purposeful.

- **Be brave.** Don't be afraid to take a stand for what you believe is right, even if everyone else is on the other side. Be true to your convictions.

- **Remember there are no shortcuts.** You learn only by doing something, doing it again, and doing it once more.

- **Say thank you.** Too many journalists have forgotten this basic rule of life. When someone helps you, thank him or her. It's the right thing to do and people will remember it.

- **Raise hell.** Anger is sometimes appropriate. Don't be afraid to take a stand against the outrages in life and society.

- **Have fun.** Don't get so caught up with the grandeur of what you're doing that you lose sight of the immense joy of the work. It will end way too soon, so enjoy it while you can.

## CONCLUSION

Bearak and his colleague, British freelancer Stephen Bevan, spent four nights in dank cells before a magistrate dismissed the charges against them and they were released. In fact, "committing journalism" was no longer a crime on the books in Zimbabwe. The law had been changed a few months before, and it was illegal only to falsely claim to be accredited.

It's not a crime to commit journalism in this country, either. But what if it were? Could you get arrested? Would you be convicted, or would the evidence against you be unconvincing to a jury of your peers?

Make your part of the world a better place. Commit journalism.

## assignments

In Chapter 1, you created a list of the reasons why you want to become a journalist. Review the list now. Ask yourself these questions:

1. Are there items you would like to add or drop?
2. How has your thinking about the craft and practice of journalism changed?
3. What are your hopes and aspirations for both yourself and other journalists?
4. What can you do to make a difference in the world around you?

## notes

1. Interview with Barry Bearak, February 13, 2009; Barry Bearak, "In Zimbabwe Jail: A Reporter's Ordeal," *The New York Times,* April 27, 2008. Available online. www.nytimes.com/2008/04/27/world/africa/27bearak.html. Accessed April 14, 2011.
2. Interview with Mary Bishop, August 31, 2008.

# index

CPSIA information can be obtained at www.ICGtesting.com
Printed in the USA
BVOW082349090812

297541BV00006B/4/P